Womansoul

Letters of Encouragement and Possibility

Pat Duffy, OP

W9-AGK-971

Resurrection Press
An Imprint of
CATHOLIC BOOK PUBLISHING CO.
Totowa • New Jersey

Dedication

To my Mother:

Thank you for all the letters you wrote me

and for the love you send me every day.

First published in December 2001 by

Catholic Book Publishing/Resurrection Press

77 West End Road

Totowa, NJ 07512

Copyright © 2001 by Pat Duffy, OP

ISBN 1-878718-68-1

Library of Congress Catalog Card Number: 2001-135976

All rights reserved. No part of this book may be reproduced or transmitted in any form or by any means, electronic or mechanical, including photocopying, recording, or by any information storage and retrieval system without permission in writing from the publisher.

Cover design by John Murello

Printed in Canada

Contents

Salutation

Dear Woman of Soul:

Do you remember the first piece of mail you ever received? For many of us, the moment our mothers announced: "You have mail!" was a wondrous event. I asked several friends if they could remember the first time they received mail. I was amazed that without hesitation each had a story to tell.

Peggy recalled being about four years old. Her father was in the Navy and had sent her a letter. Peggy related her memories of the grand ceremony that accompanied the letter's arrival. She remembers cleaning out a drawer, placing the letter in it, and eagerly anticipating the letters that would follow. The drawer became a sanctuary not only for her father's letters but also for the birthday cards and other greetings that arrived throughout the years.

Liz remembers a time when she was four or five years old. She had gone to the movies with her mother and saw a contest display for the movie *Bambi*. Her mother filled out the raffle coupon for her and about one month later, long after she had forgotten about the contest, her letter arrived. Liz remembers the joy of seeing her name on the envelope from the Loew's Theatre. Enclosed was an announcement that she had won a set of Bambi buttons. The buttons were immediately sewn onto her new coat and the announcement card was framed!

I was approaching my fourth birthday when I received my first letter. It was a birthday card from my aunt with a one-dollar bill enclosed. Life was never the same after that event! I began looking for mail on a regular basis. I was delighted when someone thought of me and was willing to take the time to share something of themselves with me, particularly if a dollar bill was enclosed!

From Christmas cards to pen pal letters, we all learned the importance of taking a pen in hand and communicating with another person. The mail I receive now consists mainly of catalogs, bills, and credit card offers. In this world of email and instant messages, I am still delighted to open the mailbox and see a letter hand addressed to me. How wonderful to know that someone thought enough of me to take the time to write!

This book is a collection of letters to women. It began with a single letter I was moved to write while on a retreat several years ago. I wanted to share something of the beauty and peace I was experiencing at a Trappist Monastery in upstate New York. One evening I sat down and simply began to write to women who I knew were longing to grow in relationship with God and themselves. When I finished writing the letter, I realized that through my pen I had communicated something of my soul. Writing the letter enabled me to express what was happening within me.

Letter writing has traditionally been a means of sharing something of the writer's soul with another. Throughout history people of faith have written letters to express the ways they are both moved and led by God. From John Chrysostom to Clare of Assisi to Thomas Merton, there is a recorded history of God's activity in people's lives through the letters they wrote. Present-day readers of these letters can enter into the experience of the writer's spiritual life as well as the relationship they shared with the one they were addressing.

So much of this kind of communication seems to be lost in our fast-paced society, where emails can be hastily sent and just as quickly deleted. In order to truly absorb the contents of a "real" letter, you must read and re-read it. I am not the sentimental type and have a tendency to dispose of letters long before I have let them rest within me. I have, however, saved one letter for over thirty years.

When I first entered the religious life, we were allowed visitors only once a month. Mail arrived twice weekly. My mother always made sure that I received a letter from her on mail days. She would keep me abreast of all that was happening in the lives of my family and friends. My father, on the other hand, never wrote to me. He was a quiet man of few words who would point out that he didn't write because my mother had already told me everything. I was genuinely surprised one mail day to see my father's handwriting on an envelope. In the enclosed letter, he summed up our relationship in a few words, and in the process gave me a treasure. My father has been dead for over twenty years now, but every once in a while I take out his letter and read it. I am instantly reconnected with my father and all the love he brought into my life. Those few words are a long-ago gift that keeps giving me something of this great man's heart and soul.

The letters that follow are from my heart and soul to yours. They are expressions of my struggle to grow into wholeness and to share the many ways I meet God in everyday life. They are also filled with wisdom I have gleaned through listening to women who long for "something more" in their lives. There is one letter for each month of the year. I encourage you to spend time reflecting on each letter and making it your own by using the Soul Suggestions given at the end of each. These are just suggestions that are intended to facilitate your reflection. You may discover other channels to open your soul to the grace of this present moment. If you gather with other women who search for more, you could use the letters as a common reflection. Above all, have fun with them!

Many women have contributed to the heart and soul of these letters. Michele Del Monte, my soul friend with whom I share a house, a ministry, and the ups and downs of life, has been the strength behind my writing, telling me, "It is time to put your feet to the fire and do it!" She has never tired of listening to a letter or celebrating when each one was completed. My dear friend, Sister Philomena O'Brien, OSU of St. Ursula's Center, Blue Point, NY provides the location and hospitality for my Wednesday night gatherings of women. These women provide the wisdom, truth, humor, and encouragement for my ministry as a preacher. Jane Vigliotta, my friend and colleague, has painstakingly made these letters readable. Jane is never afraid to say, "What do you mean when you say that?" The spoken word is a preacher's tool, and Jane has helped to transform my spoken word into the written word. Emilie Cerar, my editor at Resurrection Press, encouraged me to write these letters and believed that I would actually do it. Emilie delivers these letters to you. To all of these women, I give my heartfelt thanks.

Finally, my golden retrievers, Friar and Willow the Wonder Dog, listened to and labored through each letter. They never let me take myself too seriously, and are very pleased that these letters have been sent, for now there is more time for petting and playing!

In these letters I offer you something of my soul as a gift. I pray that through my sharing you will be encouraged to enter more deeply into your own soul. There, through the truth of your life, may you grow in grace, peace, and the love of your God.

Sister Pat

January

NEW YEAR, NEW HEART

Dear Woman of Soul:

We have just walked across a year, and like a Clint Eastwood character, we can see that there has been "the good, the bad, and the ugly." Hopefully, there has also been a touch of the delightful.

New Year's Day is a good time to look back over the past year and make resolutions to grow. I always become concerned when I hear someone speak of New Year's resolutions as if they are a correction of our behavior instead of a call to new life.

The other night we had a big snowstorm and our neighbors went outside with a yardstick to measure the amount of snow that had fallen. How many times have your New Year's resolutions been the measuring sticks to see how you are doing? It's good to remember that God invites us not to measure our progress or our faults, but to always begin anew in our journey to the fullness of life.

Grace—the love of God moving in our lives—is not given to us because we have performed well in life. It is a free gift, no strings attached. Grace is the movement of God's vision in our lives. When we respond to grace, we are responding to the way God wants us to live. This is always a call to life!

In Isaiah: 43:19 we hear our God crying out, "I am doing a brand new thing. Can you not see it?" These challenging words have nothing to do with measuring and everything to do with responding in trust and hope. As I was looking at journal entries I had written over a period of five years, I realized that I referred to this quote twenty-one times! I was astonished and I began to laugh. For years God had been telling me something *I did not see.* Now I have moved into living the "new thing" without knowing it. So much for years of study on the spiritual life!

We do sometimes just slip into newness, but we generally need a little push. When my disabled golden retriever was a puppy, we began to see a new veterinarian. He is a special man who is devoted to both his canine clients and their owners. His interest in our dog's special needs touches me deeply. His openness to exploring both traditional and non-traditional treatments always keeps my hope alive for my beloved pet. It was obvious, however, that the doctor was both constrained and overworked in the clinic where he was practicing.

My roommate Michele and I suggested and even prodded him to begin his own practice. He definitely wanted to do it, but it just wasn't happening. Meanwhile, people continued to choose him over other staff members as their pet's doctor. He had a "practice-in-waiting," but he failed to see it.

Everything changed when he met Joni. They fell in love, and her love gave him a new vision that changed his life. They are now married and have a large and thriving practice in a neighboring town.

Life is all about being open to love and the vision that God, who is Love, has for us. This involves taking a risk and trusting that God will indeed be with us. Ask yourself, "Has God been faithful to me?" Perhaps your life has not turned out the way you planned, but has God been there for you? If the answer is "Yes," then you can step out in courage with the personal conviction that God will continue to be faithful in your life.

To take more risks in life, we need to look at life from different perspectives. Sometimes we are held back by one-way vision. I often suggest to people that they get a kaleidoscope and take the time to view familiar people and things through it. It is like a journey into the unexpected. The most familiar objects can take on a magical image when we shift our perspective.

For some of us, seeing with a new vision can be a gift of wonder. For others, however, it may be a very frightening experience. If your expectations of life are very high, you may be shaken by a shift in vision. "Expecters," myself included, are people who work hard, are deeply committed, and *expect* certain results from their labor. After all, we know what is best! This attitude is a feeble attempt to control our life situations and can lead to great disappointments and dashed hopes.

An example of this "expecting" attitude is my insistence on having a real Christmas tree. Several years ago even though I had recently suffered multiple injuries from a car accident and found myself bedridden for the holidays, I *expected* to have a real tree. As friends labored for hours to decorate the largest tree they could fit into my house, I struggled with my need to arrange the lights and garland myself. I inevitably found myself supervising every visitor in the rearrangement of the ornaments from my sickbed. Still, the tree did not live up to my expectations and was undressed and out of the house by December 28.

This year we decided a real tree might be just too much to handle with our puppy. Since she brings pine branches into the house for snacks, a tree might be mistaken for a real feast! Instead we purchased a 9-foot, pre-lit tree. I *expected* that it would need a little help from me, since it had only white lights. I *expected* that it would need at least 300 colored lights added to its 1,400 white lights, to meet my personal Christmas tree standards. After a quick and easy assembly, we plugged in the tree and stepped back to pass judgment. In a quick shift of vision, Michele and I together uttered "Ah" in wonderment of the beautiful spectacle before us. I am astonished that someone figured out how to make a perfect artificial Christmas tree without any help from me! In a kaleidoscope moment I realized that wonders truly never cease. The lesson of the "make-believe" tree is to see life as the gift that it is rather than to hold ourselves captive to a vision of how we think it should be. So much for the "expecters"!

How important it is for us to realize that our vision of life is shaped by the choices we make. Day in and day out our choices shape our destiny. The life we are living is a direct result of the choices we have made in response to life's situations. Courageous choices are conscious choices. When we are in tune with God's vision and decide to choose life, there is an awareness of what we are choosing. We leave ourselves open to the possibility that God is inviting us to move into a brand new thing. When we are caught up in life's "crazies," our choices tend to be unconscious and often destructive to our souls. We can find ourselves saying things like: "I will break his heart if I take that job."

"I can't move away from my mother." "What will people say if I do that?" These choices speak of a fear of disappointing others rather than following a vision of life. We are acting in conflict with our own desires and may find ourselves living other people's lives. Courageous choices—no matter how small—build us up for the big decisions in life. They keep us on a path of paying attention to how God is directing our lives.

A wise friend once told me that you need only three things to have great peace. First, you need to know that someone loves you. Second, you need to know that you are doing something worthwhile. And, third, you need to have something to look forward to. These words have served me well. When I feel out of sorts and not connected with a strong and good vision for my life, I look at these three statements to decide where I need to open myself to the flow of God's grace.

To be open to grace takes time and quiet. These two things are so difficult to fit into our days, but they are the paths to fullness of life. The prophet Elijah heard the voice of the Lord in a whisper. God's vision for us does have its time, and it will not delay. It may come directly or through a messenger like Joni; but there is one thing we can be sure of—it will come!

Happy New Year!

Sister Pat

Soul Suggestions

Week One

What or whose opinion have you used as a standard of measure in your life?

Do you want to make any changes?

Why not buy a small plastic ruler and carry it in your purse? When you feel you are ready, break it. How does it feel?

Week Two

Make a list entitled, "I expect . . . " and then write your expectations. Let the list grow as long as you need it to be. Look at it several times during the week. Are other people involved in your expectations? Should they be informed; or, would it be better to invite their input?

Week Three

This week why not buy yourself a small kaleidoscope. They are available for less than a dollar at most party stores. Take some time to use it to look at the familiar people and things in your life. Is there room for change in your vision?

Week Four

Set aside some time this week to reflect on the following keys to happiness:

Do you know you are loved? By whom?

Are you doing something that is worthwhile to you?

What are you looking forward to?

February

KEEPING COMPANY WITH GOD

Dear Woman of Soul:

We have all known "an Emma" at some time in our lives. The Emma I know was a classmate of mine during my high school years. She was the kind of girl who never seemed to fit in with the crowd. In the 1960's when it was the rage to wear tie-dyed clothing, Emma was wearing bobby socks and saddle shoes. She was excluded from the plans made by most of the kids; and basically, I felt sorry for her. Soon I was making an effort to include Emma in any gathering I had with my friends.

When I entered the convent after high school, there were very strict visiting rules. Friends were only allowed to visit twice a year; and they all had to come on the same day. Visiting days were very hectic and noisy, as all the visitors were gathered in one large auditorium. Many of my friends would come to see me, but there was one friend who I always knew would be there—Emma. She would sit quietly while my other friends and I carried on. We had so much to say after a six-month separation that our visits often seemed like talking marathons. Emma, however, was a quiet spectator.

I called Emma several years later when I was planning to go to a university in California for a summer graduate program. I needed someone to take me to the airport and pick me up six weeks later when I returned. She happily agreed to do both. On the evening that I returned, I was walking from the gate area when I saw a young woman approaching. She looked familiar but certainly not like the Emma I knew. She was dressed in a beautiful floral outfit, her hair looked lovely, and she was beaming. I wanted to ask, "What happened to you?" but before I could say anything, she began to tell me about Mark. Apparently Emma met him the day after I left for California. For the next hour I listened to how wonderful Mark was and how much he loved her.

This incident made me think about the expression "keeping company," which I often heard as a child. My parents frequently spoke about the days when they were "keeping company" and what they did and didn't do. Isn't "keeping company" a wonderful phrase? Do you remember keeping company with someone? What was it like? How did it feel? What was it like to be separated from that person for even a short period of time?

Origen, one of the earliest Fathers of the Church, described prayer as "keeping company with God." This extraordinary definition of prayer brings us right to the heart of what it truly is. Prayer is not speaking or acting—it is a relationship. The Baltimore Catechism supports that definition of prayer. Those of us who are old enough will recall that to the question, "What is prayer?" we memorized the response, "Prayer is the lifting of our minds and hearts to God." Take a moment to think about that. Not only our minds but also our hearts are involved in our movement toward God. We also memorized the different kinds of prayer. The letters A C T S helped us to recall that they are adoration, contrition, thanksgiving, and supplication. Let's look at each of these categories *vis-a-vie* prayer as a relationship.

Adoration. Isn't affirming the other person important in any relationship? Through adoration we recognize the greatness of the Divine Presence in our lives. When we invite God into our lives through prayer, we are acknowledging and affirming the relationship we share. This is the most intimate relationship we can have. God is all about lovemaking. We have the opportunity to invite this great lover to share each moment of our lives. As in any other relationship, keeping company with God means always being aware of His presence. With every step we take, the One who loves us is our companion. Rather than adoring a God who is distant and remote, we are invited to enter into the present moment with a lover who never leaves and never disappoints. Keeping company with God is all about living in the here and now.

Contrition. When we have offended someone with whom we are in relationship, we need to ask that person for forgiveness in order to sustain the relationship. Think about a time in your life when you have had to say the words "I'm sorry." Think also about a time when you have received the gift of someone's apology. We sometimes forget that as in any other relationship, our actions are important to God. The Divine does not relate to us from a distance. Through the Incarnation, the birth of Jesus, we are invited into a personal love relationship with our God—a God who longs for us. When is the last time you told God that you were sorry? What a gift you have to give to your Creator!

Thanksgiving. As small children we learned the importance of saying "thank you." I remember my niece, Olivia, struggling to say these simple words when she was two years old. She soon learned that giving and receiving is a complete circle and that the circle is bound together by a spirit of thanksgiving. We may sometimes take our loved ones for granted and not complete the circle with our thanks. We allow ourselves to be vulnerable when we give thanks by acknowledging that we need and appreciate the giftedness that someone has extended to us. We are all quick to turn to God in times of crisis. To complete the circle in our relationship with God, we need to remember to say the simple words, "thank you."

Supplication. When we are in need, we turn to the people we trust the most. I remember being in the ICU the morning after my car accident. I needed to know the truth about my condition. Although I had a number of visitors and health professionals around me, I could not bring myself to ask the question that was burning in my heart. When my friend Michele arrived, I quietly asked her, "Do I have legs?" My need to hear the truth had to be expressed to someone I trusted with my life. I am not sure if I could have received a negative answer from anyone else. When Michele looked at me and said, "Yes," I was so relieved to hear her reply. She warned me, though, that I would have to work hard to regain the use of my legs. My need for truth was also a need for companionship in the struggle that was before me.

Expressing our needs is not easy to do. Many of us assume that the people we love should know our needs. We seem to believe that our relatives and friends have a crystal ball that reveals our needs; therefore, we have no reason to express our vulnerability. I cannot tell you how often I hear wives say, "He should know what I need." This mentality is a way of avoiding rejection. We do the same thing with God. Of course, God knows our needs, but we must invite Him into our life situations by expressing our needs to Him. Pride is what prevents us from doing this. When we fail to express our needs, we fail to be vulnerable to our loved ones and our God.

Many of us learned "our prayers" as small children. I am sure some of you can still recite the "Angel of God" today. Formal prayers, words written by another, are important in our communal prayer experiences. When we come together to pray, we need words that can be said together to express our unity as a faith community. If our prayers are exclusively formal, however, our relationship with God will also be formal.

When I think about prayer, I am reminded of Tevye, the main character from *Fiddler on the Roof*. He held nothing back in his relationship with God. He yelled and screamed. He whined and cried. In other words, he had a real relationship with God. Each time Tevye was confronted by a dilemma, he turned to God. In his own boisterous and emotional way, Tevye was indeed keeping company with God.

Not all of us have this type of personality. It is not essential that we do. What is essential is that each of us be who we truly are with our God. For some of us devotional prayers such as the rosary or novenas support our faith life. These are like favorite stories or memories that we share with special people in our lives. Although stories and memories are important, relationships cannot thrive on these alone. There must be interaction in the present moment. Tevye demonstrates one way to relate to God in the present moment when he goes up on the roof and exclaims, "Would it be so bad God, if . . . " There he is having a person-to-person moment with his God.

Some people have great devotion to a particular saint. St. Anthony, the patron saint of lost things, is probably the most popular. Many others, including the Little Flower, St. Francis, and St. Jude are also favorite saints for various needs. For many years I did not understand why people would pray to a saint when God is always available. Wouldn't we only need a saint to intercede on our behalf if our God was distant and remote? I recently met a woman named Sally who shared with me her perspective about devotion to the saints. Sally had experienced a time of great depression. She had gone through a nasty divorce and was very lonely. One day Sally came across a book about the lives of the saints. Each day she read about one saint and invited that saint to come and sit with her in the darkness. Sally was not asking the saint to intercede with God, but rather to share his/her humanity with her. After all, she told me, they were people who knew the joys and pains of being human. It was through the presence of the saints that Sally found herself being lifted from her personal darkness. What a wonderful experience!

Why not study a saint's life and then invite that person to be a companion for you. This type of devotional prayer brings together the communion of saints, both living and dead, who are people of faith.

Another life-giving form of prayer is giving our imagination over to God. I remember sitting in a hot classroom late in May as a small child. The flowers were all in bloom and the breeze was carrying the songs of birds. I looked out the window and felt myself float away. Sister Dolores Mary jolted me back to reality when she hit my desk with a ruler and told me to stop daydreaming. What a pity! Daydreaming was such a wonderful escape from that hot classroom.

How often have we been told to stop daydreaming? Why? Is evil stored in our imagination? Actually, within our imagination rests all the possibilities that God has given us for our lives. Why not invite God to speak to you through your imagination? Guided imagery tapes are readily available and can be very helpful. You can also simply sit back, close your eyes, and imagine yourself taking a walk with your God. What does God say to you? How do you respond? What places in your life would you like to share with God? This form of prayer is deeply intimate and personal. It also opens us up to the unexpected. When we give God space in our lives, we can be sure that God will fill it with Divine Presence.

My friend Emma taught me a great lesson about keeping company. She and Mark have been married for 27 years. Times have not always been good, but through their years together they have worked at keeping company and they have upheld one another with love. Faithfulness is essential in a love relationship.

Last month I asked you to reflect on whether God has been faithful. If you can now answer "yes," then with trust rooted in your experience, you can move into the "more."

Sister Pat

Soul Suggestions

Week One

If your prayer were made visible, what would it look like? Spend some time with this question. Allow it to enter your heart, and then visualize your response. Why not use a piece of paper and a few crayons to color your response?

Week Two

By what name do you call God? Sit quietly for a few minutes and allow this name to move from your heart to your lips. Repeat the name softly until you feel it moving through you. This is your personal mantra. Use your mantra anytime you need to bring to consciousness the power of God's love for you.

Week Three

A song from the musical *Godspell* says, "I'll put a pebble in my shoe." This was to be a reminder of walking with God. This week look for a symbol of how you are walking with God. Display the symbol so that it will catch your attention at unexpected moments.

Week Four

Is there someone who has helped you see God's love in your life? This week might be a good time to give thanks for this person. Why not affirm this person's goodness by writing a note of thanks?

March

ENTER THE MAGIC

Dear Woman of Soul:

"Ready for a big adventure?" That's how my father summoned us for an outing—most of the time to an amusement park. Although he never went on any of the rides, my father always seemed to enjoy himself. Rye Beach Playland was one of our favorite destinations. Among the usual roller coasters and bumper cars was an "authentic" haunted house.

My first experience of the haunted house took place when I was about five years old. My father told me to go in with my older brothers and they would take care of me. This from a man who had nine older brothers! When we entered the house, I was very frightened and the trip no longer seemed like a big adventure. My brothers compounded my fear by making all sorts of scary noises. I trembled as skeletons popped out of dark corners and bats flew overhead.

Halfway through the attraction we walked out onto a small balcony. At that point I grabbed onto the railing and became paralyzed. This started a big adventure of another kind! The employees had to get an extension ladder and climb up to rescue me. When my rescuer reached me, he had to pry my little fingers off the railing. Only after they safely returned me to my father's arms did I start to cry. That day I made a decision that has affected my whole life. I decided I would never let fear rule me again. On our next trip to Rye Playland, I was the first to enter the haunted house.

I am sure many of you have experienced fearful times in your lives and know deeply the struggle not to let fear rule you. We have probably all stood at some time in our lives on a metaphorical balcony, holding onto the railing with a death grip, just hoping someone would come and free us.

There is good news for all of us who have known this intense fear. We read in the Book of the Prophet Isaiah: "You are to be a crown of splendor in the hand of God, a royal diadem. No longer are you to be named forsaken or abandoned, but you shall be called my delight." No matter how forsaken we might feel, God is companioning us. We are not abandoned. We are God's delight! These are powerful words to hold on to during dark days.

I remember a period of time during my late twenties when I was very unhappy. Nothing seemed right in my life and I was not sure what direction to take. I sought advice from a sister in my community who was older and I thought, wiser than I. Our conversation was devastating to me. She proceeded to tell me everything that was wrong with me and how I could change. I walked out of that meeting feeling overwhelmed and hopeless. Two years later I made a weeklong silent retreat with God as my director. During that retreat many of the same issues arose in my prayer time. Rather than feeling fearful and hopeless, I experienced what the prophet Isaiah was saying. I came to understand that with all my flaws I was still God's delight. Fear has no place in the love of God.

As far as adventures go, the journey inward is one of the biggest. For many of us, though, it is riddled with fear. I recently spent some time with a woman who literally cannot sit still. She is obviously afraid of what she may hear in the stillness; therefore, she just keeps moving. During our conversation I came to realize that this woman views the inner journey much the same as I did the haunted house on my first visit. I encouraged her to let go of the railing she was gripping and enter the magic of knowing she is God's delight. She looked at me like I was nuts! I don't think she is ready to leave the balcony yet!

The journey inward is magical. It is beyond our control and filled with wonders and yes, skeletons that pop out at us. But they can be faced. As in an old Irish story about a man who was being chased by a ghost, it was only when the man was exhausted and turned and faced the ghost that it disappeared. Knowing that we are the delight of God, we can face fear with courage, a gift of the Holy Spirit that abides in each of us. Until we come face to face with the ghosts or skeletons, we won't know it is within us.

Thomas Merton, a twentieth century mystic, often spoke about this journey inward. He believed that when we come to the true self, we find God there. The Divine Presence rests in our personal truth. This inner journey to the true self is long and often hazardous to all the "selves" we have portrayed to others in our life. In reality, we have to decide sometime whether or not to take the journey, whether to go for the big adventure or stand frozen in fear on some balcony.

There are many obstacles on the inner journey. Probably the most difficult is letting go of the masks we have worn for other people. So many of us have performed life rather than lived it. I have heard women say, "I don't know who to be in that situation." Why not just be yourself? Others' expectations of who we should be can obstruct our inner journey. You may be fearful that you will no longer be accepted or liked. That is a risk you take on this journey. But if God is directing us and we walk as God's delight, then we must stay true to who we are at our center. A word of advice: Make sure you truly know that God is the one directing you. You will know this through your personal honesty and by checking it out with a spiritually mature person or two.

March is still in the beginning of a new year, and we are still in the early years of a new century. It is our moment in time and we need to decide how we are going to live it. During this month the trees model for us how to live. They finally let go of those last few dead leaves that they stubbornly held on to through the long, cold winter. Now they can make way for new life. What do you want to take with you into this new time? What do you want to let go of as you step across the threshold? We carry a lot of stuff around with us that we simply don't need, such as the old tapes that play in our heads. Some of the voices have long been dead, but they still seem to control us. If we are dragging these tapes around with us, how are we going to enter the big adventure? Maybe now is the time to erase the tapes and replace them with the words of our God, "You are my delight!"

The opinions of others can cripple us on the journey. When we are worried about, "What will they think?" we are letting fear take over. And truly, what does it matter what they think? Let's take the neighbors, for instance. So many of us are concerned about what the neighbors will think when we don't really know or even speak to most of them. If we are bringing everybody's opinion of us into this new time, it is not going to be new at all—it will just be more of the old. Do you want to bring these opinions with you, or is now the time to leave them on the doorstep as you go forward?

Do you want to be fully alive or do you just want to live? To enter the magic is to trust God with our very lives. This will only happen when our desire for life is larger than our fear. It means we have to make a decision to embrace the adventure of being God's delight. We need to make this decision at every season of our lives.

I knew a wonderful sister who lived to be 106. She lived each day as an adventure. When she was 100 years old, she had only one birthday wish. She wanted the Mets baseball team to come to her party. Well, a large number of the players did come and they made her a Met for a day. She even got a jacket and a hat. It was a great celebration. At the end of the day she said to me: "I guess some people think I'm an old fool." I responded, "Well, if they do, at least you're a happy old fool!" She erupted in laughter.

Living a magical adventure does not mean having more stuff. Do we really need more stuff? I love to shop and it can make you feel good for a while, but there is something more fulfilling. Being in the adventure is about living fully, tasting each mouthful, feeling each tear, listening to each joy, and never letting a moment pass you by.

The maps of the past may not give the best directions for the present. Many of us are still carrying maps of who we should be and how we should act. Too many of our maps were printed with fear already in place. Ancient mapmakers, or cartographers, only drew maps of the known world. They left the unknown lands out and would write around the border, "there be dragons, there be dragons!"

Would it really be an adventure if there were no dragons? The good news is that women know what to do about the dragons and monsters. We put the light on! That is what the journey is all about. When we turn on the light of truth and courage, we find ourselves in a most magical place. This place is the kingdom of God, and the path is marked with signs of welcome. The signs say: "Maureen, you are my delight," "Stacey, you are my delight," and "Jenny, you are my delight." Look close, there is a sign with your name on it.

To each of us the God of the adventure is beckoning. We are being called home, home to the center. Enter in without fear and enjoy yourself.

Sister Pat

Soul Suggestions

Week One

Make a map of what has been given to you in your life. Include the limitations that have been placed on you, the different selves you have portrayed to people, and the tapes you have heard.

Week Two

What balcony are you standing on while gripped with fear? Be with this.

Week Three

Draw a new map. Become the cartographer of your big adventure. What do you want to take from the old map? What do you want to leave behind?

Week Four

Every time you flip on a light switch, remember the light and God's words, "You are my delight."

April

BE THE M-A-G-I-C

Dear Woman of Soul:

Have you ever felt a little off balance, not sure which direction to go in? That is how I once felt on another big family adventure to my favorite amusement park, Rockaway Playland, when I was about seven years old. In addition to the usual rides, it also had Davey Jones' Locker. The attraction was shaped like a ship, and the floors and everything in it were slightly tilted. It was supposed to simulate a shipwreck at the bottom of the sea. In this most magical place, the mirrors distorted your shape and fish floated by as you struggled to keep your balance. I just loved to go in it because your perception of things was changed by the slight slant on which everything was fixed.

My cousin, Janice, often came with us on our big adventures. Although she loved the rides, she was afraid to go into Davey Jones' Locker. You see, the outside of the building had a series of mirrors, much like the ones inside, that distorted your shape. Janice found them frightening because she felt like someone was changing the way she saw things. This made her terribly uneasy.

We, too, can become uneasy when we feel that we are not in control of things in our lives. That is why anything to do with "magic" scares some people. Webster tells us: "Magic is a sense that there is a supernatural power at work." This does not necessarily mean something that is negative or evil. I love magic! It means I don't have to do or be everything. It can be transforming in our lives when we open ourselves to all the magic God can be for us. God can even transform the way we see things; and a transformation of the way we see things causes a change in perception, that in turn, brings about a change in our attitude.

The month of April hints at many of the magical aspects of nature. The once-bare tree branches begin to turn light green with life. The clouds water the earth, and the earth in response produces miracle sprouts of hope. Bulbs planted long ago struggle to leave the darkness of the earth in response to the light. God's supernatural power is at work, waking up the earth; and you can almost hear the earth saying YES!

This month may be an excellent time for us to plant seeds of magical attitudes in our own hearts. I would like to share with you some thoughts that may lead you to have a magical attitude, one that can help you to believe that there is a supernatural power, God, at work in your life. But beware, some of your perceptions may be altered and you may even begin to change some attitudes! Our MAGIC attitudes are: Mindfulness, Awe, Grace, Integrity, and Continuation.

In the journey to be the magic, we have to make decisions along the way. The first decision is to have an attitude of mindfulness. This can be quite difficult because it means living in the present moment. If you are like me, you might find yourself thinking about several things at once. Focusing on what is going to happen next can often obscure what is happening right now. This practice leaves us feeling frenzied and in turmoil. Being mindful means being present here and now to this moment and not allowing ourselves to be pulled between past and future moments.

The Dali Lama is the great spiritual leader of the Tibetan people, but his influence in our culture has helped many of us transform our ways to live more mindfully. One morning I awoke quite early and found my mind cluttered with many thoughts of the day ahead. I was feeling very uneasy. Then I remembered the Dali Lama's advice. He suggested that if you want peace, be peaceful. Invoke peace to come to you. I began to invoke peace, inviting it to come to me in that moment. I did this for about ten minutes; simply repeating, "I invite peace." When I got up, I felt very peaceful. In that moment I was present to peace. You see, God is always waiting to change our vision. We need only ask.

The alternative to living mindfully is living mindlessly. Just think about a day when everything went wrong. You forgot something important, you lost your car keys, and an overdue bill came in the mail. These are all results of a lack of mindfulness. I can really laugh at myself sometimes on days like this. I feel like I need a memory pill. Maybe the truth is I need a moment to call myself back to being mindful, present to the moment I am in. Mindlessness is a sign that we have missed being present in the moment. We suffer the consequences for this.

The second attitude changes the shape of our lives the way looking in a fun house mirror changes our vision. Are we going to live in *awe*, or are we going to be *absent*? We have to make a choice. If we are going to live in the magic of the supernatural power active in our lives, we will live as the delight of God. Then we will certainly be in a state of awe. We will see everything with a new vision.

Several years ago I took a group on a retreat to Hawaii. It was paradise! Each day of the retreat someone would share an experience of the beauty around us and say, "It was awesome!" From my room I looked out onto "Nurse's Beach" from the movie, *South Pacific*. The mountains, waterfalls, lush greens and flowers moved each of us to see the depths of beauty in creation. I don't think I will ever look at a flower the same way again!

In Hawaii we were overcome by the magnificence of creation. Being in awe came naturally. Once touched by awe, it is not difficult to remember it and allow the awe to bring us back to the magic of life.

Do you want to live in awe or do you choose to be absent? There are so many women who seem to absent themselves from life. One day in the food store I noticed the eyes of the cashier. They looked empty. It was like she was not home. I then began to notice other women who seemed to be absent from the moment and what they were doing. A woman pushing a child on a swing was staring off into space and her eyes were vacant. She did not appear to be daydreaming. Her eyes were blank. Another woman I observed was pushing an elderly person in a wheel-chair. She had no interaction with the person and her eyes appeared hollow as she walked along. I am so saddened to see women who seem to have moved away from themselves. I want to ask each of them, "Where are you? Where did you go?"

Yesterday I had a moment with my puppy, Willow, which brought me back to a magnificent sense of awe. We were having an early April dusting of snow. Willow was outside running and leaping, trying to grab the snow with her tongue. She was certainly present to the moment and filled with awe at the falling snow. I went outside and although I cannot run, I joined her in chasing the snowflakes and trying to catch them on my tongue. Thank God the neighbors couldn't see me! Imagine what they would have to say about that little moment of awe. It is up to you. Do you want to live in awe or do you choose to be absent?

Another important attitude concerns how we view ourselves. Do you believe that you are *graced*? You see, we either know that we are graced or we will find ourselves groping in life. I once met a woman who told me she did not know who she was and she felt so alone. This was heartbreaking to hear. She had no idea that she was the delight of God. She felt isolated and was groping for an identity. I spoke at length with her about God's promise to be with her and asked her to look at how the grace of God was in her life. Slowly, she began to discover that she was not alone. Each day she prayed to see how God was walking with her. This woman made a great discovery that shifted her vision. Rather than seeing herself as someone unloved, forgotten, and groping for attention, she awakened to being the delight of God. Believe me, this did not happen overnight, but it did happen.

My middle name is Grace. This has been a blessing in my life because it has kept me mindful of the reality of who I am. Whether we carry the name or not, we should all carry the knowledge that we are born in grace.

After opening ourselves to mindfulness, awe, and grace, we will be ready to look at our own *integrity*. Integrity is a sense of yourself as you truly are. It has nothing to do with whom your mother thinks you should be. Nor does it result from whom your husband, children, or friends think you should be. Integrity is being who God has created you to be and feeling at peace with that. After the past two months, I am sure you know who God has made you to be: a delight.

This does not mean that you are nice all the time. I think I am nice about forty percent of the time. I am working on raising that percentage, but I'm still ok. No one is perfect and we are all in the process of becoming. The difficulty lies in feeling we must act a certain way. In truth, there are certain behaviors that are appropriate for particular situations. Too many of us, however, have become prisoners of other people's expectations. I am a religious sister. You would be surprised at the number of opinions there are on how a good sister should behave. You would be even more surprised at how many people feel the need to tell you their opinion. When I experience this, I try to be patient and understanding; but I do get annoyed.

One day after I had given a presentation, a 25-year-old woman approached me. She asked me why I was not wearing a habit. This is a question I hear often and I was a little impatient with her. I told her that I did not understand why she was asking that question when I had not worn a habit during her entire lifetime. She told me that she had seen Whoopi Goldberg in *Sister Act*. I burst into laughter and told her that although I enjoyed the movie, this was not an image I aspired to.

If you are not at home within yourself, you will be quite indecisive. Making decisions will be a struggle because you will always be concerned about whether others accept you. Find your integrity. Live it—even if the neighbors don't like it. You will be amazed to find that as you start to like who you are, others will also begin to like you.

And finally, when you are the magic and all its qualities are alive within you, something very special will happen. You will have the ability to *continue* on. We women need the magic in order to be and do all that is necessary in our lives. The greatest sign of such a woman is her ability to get up after a devastating time and attend to what needs tending. She can carry on. This is what changes us from girls to women. We can move outside our own pain, without ignoring it, to tend to life.

My cousin stood outside Davey Jones' Locker because she was afraid it would change how she saw things. It is very sad when a woman ignores the power of God's magic because she is afraid. These women often get stuck in life roles that do not fit them and often decide to absent themselves from life. Then their life falls apart because they make the same mistakes again and again. I once met a woman who told me she married the same man three times. I was shocked and asked her why. She said that she had searched and found the same man in three different packages. Time and again she looked for men who would abuse her. What a collision path she was on! Another woman told me that she was raised by an alcoholic father and had become so used to it that she eventually chose to marry a man who was also an alcoholic.

Grasp the magic of God's love in your life. Be the magic so that you will live with mindfulness and a sense of awe, knowing that you are graced. Then you will have a rich sense of integrity and a great ability to carry on.

Have a delightful month watching the earth open to God's magic!

Sister Pat

Soul Suggestions

Week One

Each day this week set aside five minutes for quiet. During the
quiet, invoke a quality that you need in order to sustain your
peace. Gently call this quality to yourself.

Week Two

Write a list of five things that distract you from being mindful.
Now pick one that you would like to put in better balance in
your life. Each day this week, attend to making this a reality.

Week Three

Call someone you know who is having a difficult time and invite
him/her to tea. Why not share the magic with them?

Week Four

Choose a place in your home that you would like to make more
your own. Set it up to reflect peace and comfort. Each day
take a few minutes to sit there and settle in to being at home
with yourself.

May

THE CALL TO LIFE

Dear Woman of Soul:

Have you ever felt an indescribable yearning deep within you that persists even in your happiest moments? Some women have shared with me the awareness that they are being called to a deeper dimension but they do not know how to respond.

May is a month that embodies the call to new life. During this month the earth begins to show signs of all that is to come, while still clinging to the rain and chill. We sense that we are moving toward a time of beauty and abundance. Many of us begin our spring cleaning and discard the old to make room for the new life around and within us.

Although I like the concept of spring cleaning, it usually remains a fantasy in my life. I do, however, try to take time each spring to honor the yearning for new life that abides within me. I might plant Morning Glory seeds in little paper cups, place them on a sunny windowsill, and then wait for them to break through the soil. This month I would like to share with you some of my reflections on LIFE lived abundantly. Let us take the word apart and see what unfolds from within it.

Longing. Within all living things is a great longing for everything life has to offer. When I, the youngest in my family turned 35, my Mom had just turned 70. At my birthday gathering she announced, "Now we are all middle aged!" What wonderful words from a woman who rejoices daily in the gift of life! This desire for life speaks of a yearning that impels many of us to seek out "the more," to take risks, to grow beyond our own imaginings. I believe this is a response to the grace of God's possibility for our lives. This longing is a sacred thing. It connects us with the Divine who became flesh and dwelt among us, our God who resides not in a far-off heaven but rather within us. This longing is a restlessness similar to that experienced by the great mystics who longed to be taken up in love by God, the Great Lover. Such is the intimacy that is at the heart of longing.

Perhaps your longing has revealed itself in a desire to retreat to a beach house for a few days. I encourage you, however, to go deeper within and travel with your longing to its source. I once heard Marion Woodman, the renowned Jungian psychologist, describe soul as the speck of Divinity that is held captive within our humanity and is always longing for home. Take a few minutes to think about this. Are her thoughts speaking to your longing? If not, begin by spending some time at a beach house. At least you'll get a rest!

Intuition. Close your eyes for a moment and say softly to yourself: "I know." Repeat the phrase several times, and with each repetition let the words go deeper within. Do this now.

We women really do know what we know. The difficulty lies in that we do not trust the little voice that speaks to our hearts. If we are somewhat psychologically healthy, that voice will be the voice of wisdom. Most of us seem to have an innate wisdom that can help direct our lives when we honor it. We can also suffer the consequences of ignoring it. One example of this is a friend of mine who was walking down the aisle on her wedding day and heard a voice within her say, "This is not right." She subsequently spent twelve unhappy years trying to disprove her intuition!

We basically absorb only about half of what goes on around us. We then give our own meaning to what we have absorbed. Intuition is essential in that it provides a foundation for meaning in our lives. Think for a moment about a time in your life when your little voice spoke deeply to your heart. Did you listen? If not, why not? So often the "why not" is based upon how we think we should act. Someone or something external has placed an expectation on us that is in direct opposition to what we believe deep within ourselves.

Again, close your eyes for a moment and softly repeat the words "I know" to yourself until you can feel them deep within your soul. You have begun a new ritual of honoring your own sense of intuition.

Forgiveness. Forgiveness is one of the most essential attitudes for living with a peaceful spirit. It is a gift of the Spirit that we must persistently pray for before it begins to flow deep within us. Many of us have family members and friends who frequently step on our toes. Although we might be annoyed and angry about their behavior, we can often overlook and readily excuse their behavior without feeling deeply hurt or wronged. I like to think of these people as the thorns that go along with the many roses we are given in life. They are here and they are ours! So embrace them ever so carefully.

Being seriously wronged is quite another matter. In these instances the deep hurt seems to dent our souls. We learn to live with the pain, but we are never quite the same. These are the times when we need the grace of forgiveness. Don't be surprised, however, if you can't forgive instantly. It usually doesn't happen that way. We need to enter into the process of forgiving, which, believe it or not, begins with getting angry. So many women learned in our homes or in Sunday school that anger is a sin. Actually, unjustified anger that is acted upon is a sin. The deep emotional response to being wronged is anger, and it is justified.

When I went through the legal process of settling a lawsuit after my car accident some years ago, my attorney asked me to sign a paper that said no one was at fault. While I understood this was standard procedure, I did not want to sign it. Someone was at fault, and I was not the one! The young man was speeding when he lost control of his car, crossed over into my lane and hit me head-on. I was innocent and I was angry. Many months passed before my attorney was able to convince me to sign the settlement papers. Although the settlement helped with many bills, what I really wanted but never received was an apology.

The wonderful thing about forgiveness is that it does not hinge on whether the person who wronged you is repentant. When they are sorry, we have the power and can graciously forgive them; however, most of us never receive an apology when we have been wronged. In these situations we have been robbed of something and forgiveness is the only way we can take back that piece of ourselves.

Forgiveness is a grace that is given first to the forgiver and then to the forgiven, if they are open to accepting it. When we forgive, we show the other person that they no longer have power over us. We are reclaiming our power. I once read about a mother whose daughter had been murdered. After a long period of anguish, she forgave the young man who had killed her daughter. The woman said she had to forgive him in order to restore her own peace. She would not let him have two victims. What a woman and what a response to grace!

When we forgive someone, we are actually letting go of what we might perceive as our right for revenge. We really do not have such a right, but when our heart is in pain, revenge is often what keeps our adrenaline pumping. On the other hand, forgiveness produces peace and peace softens our hearts.

Some wrongs are simply intolerable. Forgiving these wrongs does not make them tolerable; it only makes them forgiven. Many women live with childhood memories of being physically or sexually abused. These horrific experiences often happened at the hands of a trusted adult, thus as a child they felt powerless. As women they are no longer powerless. Forgiving the betrayer is taking back the power, taking back the self. This act brings great freedom in the face of such painful memories. Let me reiterate that this does not happen all at once. First you must acknowledge the offense and place the blame. This is the beginning of the process of forgiving.

I know a woman whose adult life was tortured by horrible childhood memories of the abuse she suffered at the hands of her uncle. The adult she told at the time about the abuse did not believe her. She, therefore, suppressed it. As we all know, this does not work. When you keep something this painful inside yourself, some kind of sickness will occur because it has to come out somewhere. For many years my friend reacted to small offenses with uncontrollable bouts of anger. Finally one day she had had enough. She went down to her basement, took an ax and chopped an old dresser into little pieces. When she was finished, tears flowed and she resurrected from her basement with a new life. Eventually she forgave the abuser who had died fifteen years earlier. He no longer had any power over her.

This is a very dramatic story, but I believe it shows how forgiveness can move through our anger and bring us, and sometimes the offender, into a new life. If you have been seriously wronged, know that forgiveness can move through you but that it will probably take time to reach your soul. When you are on the road to forgiveness, grace is flowing within you.

Enjoy. How many of us truly enjoy ourselves? So much of our ordinary day can seem to be drudgery. I often hear people say things like, "I have to", "I must", or "I should." I seldom hear people enthusiastically say, "I'm going to", or "I want to." The following old story might have a lesson for us. There were three masons working on a project. The first one said, "I must lay these bricks." The second said, "I have to build a wall." The third said, "I'm building a cathedral!" Attitude is everything! Which mason represents your attitude toward life?

There are many party stores in my area. My favorite is named "Party Hardy." When I shop for a gathering, I like to go there because the name alone gives my attitude about the party a big boost! We need to surround ourselves with positive people and ideas.

There are so many "have to's" in our lives. Why not take some time to look at your attitudes about work and duties? Can you find something in all the "have to's" that you can really enjoy? Can you change your attitude about something you do so your day is a little more celebratory? At home we end the message on our telephone answering machine with "Have some fun today!" You should hear the responses we get! People say things like: "Maybe *you* have time for fun!" or "Fun, oh sure!" Every once in awhile I will be overjoyed to hear a message like: "I *am* going to have some fun today!"

What are you going to do with your day? How do you want your life to be? What are you going to do about it? Embracing life is similar to opening a gift. Take your time unwrapping it, but keep your heart open to what is under the wrapping. You will find fullness there.

Sister Pat

Soul Suggestions

Week One

Most people escape from something. Maybe it is more important
to escape to something. If not to a beach house, then to what
does your longing lead you?

Week Two

Each time you stop at a traffic light during this week, make it an
occasion to honor your intuition. Use the short time at the
light to repeat to yourself, "I know." Each time you say it, let
it go deeper. Why not set aside 20 minutes during this week
to press your ear to your soul and listen to what your "little
voice" is saying.

Week Three

Take a flowerpot full of potting soil. Bless it and ask God to be
with you in the moment. Write something in the soil that you
cannot forgive. Then, ask for the grace to begin living a new
life of forgiveness. Rub your hand over the dirt and let the
hurt move away from you. Finally, plant seeds in the pot and
watch them grow.

Week Four

Enjoy yourself. This week begin to change your attitude about
the things you must do. Put flowers in the kitchen, bring a
toy to work, or buy a new CD for your car. Find a way to be
surprised by joy.

June

WE ARE ALL JUST BEGINNING

Dear Woman of Soul:

Have you ever had one of those days when you wonder "How did I get myself into this?" That is exactly how I felt one autumn day as I was driving to one of our convents in upstate New York where a group of senior sisters live. These women are wonderful people. Each, in her own way, has shown me something of the beauty of living in union with God. So when they invited me to lead an evening prayer service and preach about prayer, I agreed to go although I knew I had nothing to add to their understanding of prayer.

By the time I arrived I had convinced myself that I was not up to the task. What a great attitude to have when you are already nervous! We began our prayer in the chapel. At the appointed time I got up and read from the Scriptures. Then I looked out at this small congregation of holy women and began speaking. I stumbled through my talk with some difficulty and sank back into my chair like the little girl who had just lost the spelling bee!

When the service was over each sister thanked me for sharing my thoughts with them. I was very embarrassed at their kindnesses until Sister Polycarpa approached me. She was an extraordinary woman with a delightful sense of humor. In response to her kind words of appreciation I blurted out, "Oh, Poly, what do

I have to tell you about prayer? How long have you been pray-
ing?" She replied, "Well, let me see. My mother taught me my
first prayers when I was about three years old." She was now
ninety-three years old! I said, "I have nothing to tell you. I am just
beginning." With her usual good humor and wisdom, Poly told
me, "Kid, when it comes to God, we are all just beginning."

June is a month of new beginnings. The earth is coming alive
with new life. The air is fresh, clean and warm. No wonder that
June is a very popular month for births and weddings. Our souls
seem to be bursting with newness after winter's rest and spring
showers soaking the earth. How appropriate that Sister
Polycarpa's words came to me in June. I share them with you so
that you may be encouraged to begin anew this month.

Poly's words bring great relief to many of us who feel we have
to achieve something in our prayer lives. I wonder why women
sometimes try to keep score of their prayer successes. The spiritual life is not about reaching a level of expertise in prayer but
rather about a relationship with God.

In the fourth chapter of John's Gospel, Jesus' "chance meeting" with the Samaritan woman at the well invites us into a
beginning relationship with God. I would like to share some
highlights from that story.

The woman came to the well at noon. Right away we know
there is a problem. No one in the Middle East would go to a well
at midday, when the sun is at its height. Obviously she did not
want to associate with the other women who went to the well
each day. Meanwhile, Jesus had sent his companions into town
to get provisions. He approached the well alone. When he saw

the woman, he asked for a drink. She was shocked by what she perceived to be his arrogance. No man spoke to a woman in public, especially not to a hated Samaritan woman. This woman, however, was not shy. She boldly asked Jesus why he was asking her, a Samaritan and a woman, for a drink. He responded in a most unusual way. Rather than answer her question, Jesus told her that if she knew who was asking for this drink, she would ask him for living water.

This is such a wonderful moment! Just imagine carrying a heavy stone jar to a well each day to draw the water you need. Then someone comes along and suggests that you can have living water. No more walking in the hot sun burdened by a heavy load. Now the water can come to you! We know this is not what Jesus was talking about. The woman, however, was caught up in her own moment and her own story. She missed the point.

How many of us miss the point in our spiritual lives? God is offering us living water—a symbol of the free gift of grace—and we are so caught up in our own stories about how life should be that we just don't get it. The gift is freely given, yet so often we hold to the belief that we have to earn God's love and attention.

Some of our misconceptions were born in our early religious education. I remember Sister Mary Hannah trying to explain grace to my second grade class. (If you went to Catholic school, you might have had the same lesson.) Sister drew an old-fashioned milk bottle on the blackboard and told us this represented our soul. She then took the chalk and colored in the bottle, telling us that when we did good works our souls were filled with grace. Our souls became tainted, however, when we committed a venial sin. (See, I am old!) Sister then took the eraser and made spots in the "milk." The best was yet to come! She told us that when we committed a mortal sin, our souls were emptied of grace. She demonstrated this by erasing all the chalk inside the bottle. Imagine what went through our little minds and how it affected us. The lesson was that we had to earn God's grace and could only get "refilled" if we went to confession and did penance.

If you did not hear this story, I am sure you learned some facsimile of it along the way. The point of it was that it's all up to you. The idea that God will give you grace in response to how good you are could not be further from the truth. In 1John 4:10, St. John reminds us: "It is not so much that we have loved God, but that God has first loved us." God makes the first move, and we need only respond to the great love that is given. We don't get God's attention by achieving goodness. We are already good by virtue of the very fact that God created us. What we are called to do is to respond in love and to live out of that love. Simply put, grace is the "stuff" of our love relationship with God. It is like an energy that moves between lovers. Words fail to describe it, but you know it is there. We could say that grace is our love chemistry with God. It keeps us connected with the great Lover.

If you have ever lived through a failed love relationship, you know that this energy is a "given" and cannot be achieved. All you can do is be attentive to the beloved and allow the energy to flow. Grace is much like this. Our response to God and the way we love other people is sustained by the grace relationship we share with the Lover.

Grace was the wondrous gift Jesus was offering the woman at the well. At first she missed it! Knowing that someone standing face-to-face with Jesus could miss the point of his message is very reassuring to me. It gives me comfort on the many occasions when I miss the point in my own life. Her reaction to Jesus was to become defensive and try to take control of the situation. Has that ever happened to you when you feel uncomfortable or exposed in a conversation? It did not work with Jesus. He asked the woman to go get her husband. She shot back that she had no husband. Jesus responded that she was right that she had no husband at that moment. She had had five husbands, however, and the man she was living with now was not her husband. (I always chuckle during this part of the story because I figure, at the least, Jesus was speaking to someone who was a seeker. She must have been searching for something to go through five husbands!) Jesus spoke the truth right to her heart. He wanted her to know that although he knew who she was, he still extended his life-giving waters of grace to her.

What is the truth of your life? Did you ever feel that someone would not accept you if they knew what you were really like? If so, this story is for you. I love it because the woman goes through a whole process with Jesus. She does many of the same things I have done with God. From the Samaritan woman I have learned that God is always offering me love and life. This is an important truth. None of us should be thirsting for life and love because God is always extending both to us.

Like the Samaritan woman, there is something we need to do. She had to put down her jar and look at Jesus. Her jar was the means by which she transported water. Now she had to let go of this important part of her lifestyle. Just think about all the "stuff" we carry around with us. I am a shopping bag maven. I always seem to have one with me and it is usually filled with stuff I just can't do without.

Both the jar and shopping bag are symbols for me of all the past experiences in life we seem to carry around with us. The uplifting and good experiences of our lives become part of the grace energy of our love for God and others. The negative and hurtful experiences we carry around become a burden that drags us down. Some of us, however, seem to treasure them. We keep them around to remind us how difficult life can be. Some women cannot even allow themselves to enjoy a kind word. Their response to a compliment is to go into their bag and take out something negative about themselves to counter the acknowledgement of their goodness.

A conversation with my young nephew many years ago reminds me of how we can treasure the useless and hurtful things in our lives. Shortly before Valentine's Day he had written out cute little greetings for his first grade classmates. There was one girl, however, that he wanted to give a special gift to. He was in his room looking through an old shoebox that was stuffed with what looked to me like junk. When I asked what he was doing, he told me he was trying to find something special in his treasure box to give to Jennifer. I knew Jennifer was in for a most unusual Valentine's present. He had old Coke bottle tops, a couple of broken He-man figures, some used gum, and an assortment of pennies, nickels, and broken glass from his favorite themed drinking glass. I suggested he show Jennifer the box and let her take what she wanted. He quickly snapped the box closed and

said, "Are you crazy? She might take something I want to keep."
He had a lot to learn about love!

This incident reminds me of how we can be with God. The Samaritan woman collected husbands in the hope of finding what she longed for in life. What do we collect in the hope of filling our souls? I make the same suggestion to you that I made to my nephew. Why not open your bag and show God all the stuff you have been carrying around. Then let God take what he wants. Maybe God even has a surprise to put in there for you.

Some of you may want to snap your bag closed at this suggestion, but this is what happened to the Samaritan woman. She had to put down her jar and look at Jesus. We need to do the same with anything that is keeping us from being open to God. We must put it down—let go of it. Then we, too, can look at Jesus. This is the beginning of the graced relationship. Letting go of what we are carrying makes a space for what God longs to give us. Remember, God loved us first, and that love is far greater than any "treasure" we have been identifying with in our lives. The good news is that the grace of God is always at work within us and we are continually being transformed by it. We no longer need to hold on to the hurts, fears, guilt, and anxiety that we have carried. Like the Samaritan woman, we can let go of them in the face of love.

If your response to this good news is that this must be for someone else, someone better or holier, then just think for a minute. Jesus revealed himself as the Messiah to this most unlikely woman. He found her worthy to be the first to truly know who he was in spite of all her shortcomings. It is the same for each of us. God does not measure us by our achievements. God loves us right where we are. When we respond, God calls us to abundant life.

During this season as we watch new life sprouting up all around us, take a few minutes each day to breathe in the warmth of the sun and allow it to nourish your inner life. The great St. Thomas Aquinas wrote many deep theological treatises, but I remember him for one simple line. He said, "Grace is like the air we breathe." The love energy of God is all around us, ready to animate our spirits in any given moment. St. Paul adds to that in Romans 5:2, where he tells us that it is the grace in which we now stand that allows us to hope. Take advantage of this free gift of God. Breathe deeply, that you may grow and blossom into the woman you are called to be.

One final thought! The Samaritan woman was so over-whelmed by the gift of Jesus that she ran off to tell everyone—the very people she had been trying to avoid—about him. In the process, she left her jar behind. What a wonderful beginning!

Sister Pat

Soul Suggestions

Week One

Write down on index cards all the "stuff" you have been carrying around with you. Put all the cards in a shopping bag. Throughout the month examine each card to discover what you can discard.

Week Two

Jesus offered the Samaritan woman life-giving water. As you go through the week, be mindful of every time you use water. Let it be a symbol of all that God is offering you.

Week Three

Where is the "well" in your life? When was the last time you visited your "well?" Make an appointment with yourself this week to draw life from the "well."

Week Four

Is your shopping bag emptied out? If so, celebrate and take the bag shopping with you. Buy yourself a small gift that symbolizes your growth. Put the gift in the shopping bag and bring it home.

July

WHAT DO YOU GROW?

Dear Woman of Soul:

As I see it, no matter how many things you buy, no matter how much money you make, you really only get to keep three things in life. These are the things that no one can take away from you: your experiences, your true friends, and what you grow inside yourself.

Our *experiences* in life are unique to each of us. Have you ever been at an event with a friend where you listened to the same speaker and spoke to the same people yet had a completely different experience? Just think about your family. Sometimes when we hear our brothers and sisters relate a childhood event, they seem to have been raised in different households!

Our lives are shaped by our perception of reality. Our experiences are what we hold from our perceptions. If you saw my backyard, you might think it needs a lot of work. Although that is often my experience of my yard as well, on a good day my perception allows me to just sit on the swing and experience the beauty of creation.

True friends never leave your heart. Even after years apart you can pick up a conversation right where you left off. Think for a moment about someone who is in your heart. I am sure that even the thought of that person warms you inside. A good friend gives us comfort. We are so thankful to be able to trust someone with a piece of our soul. I believe good friends show us something of the face of God.

I would like to spend some time focusing on the third aspect of what is truly our own. *What we grow inside ourselves* is a very individual and personal choice. We can grow gratitude and tenderness or bitterness and negativity. July is the month when our gardens come into full bloom. The springtime work of planting and our ongoing efforts at watering are being rewarded with an array of magical colors and delicious fruit. July, the heart of the summer, is an appropriate time to look at our inner gardens and reflect on what is growing there.

Last year Michele and I planted, weeded, pruned and marveled. This year we "Willowed!" When you have a puppy, planting takes on the dynamics of a game. Every plant in the ground provides an opportunity for digging. We thought it best not to tempt Willow beyond her power to resist. I did buy a little sunflower that I planted in what I thought would be a safe place. I don't know what happened to it, but it is gone. I do, however, have memories from previous years of planting seeds and watching them bloom. Each little plant brings with it the frustration and joy, impatience and satisfaction, defeat and glory of growth. What a wonderful image of the soul!

What do we really want to grow in our lives? There are so many books and tapes available today that profess to offer the answers to healthy psychological and spiritual growth. Every week I receive a brochure advertising another conference that promises to provide a map to the land of spiritual maturity. I am sure that they offer valuable hints and suggestions, but the reality is that we need to live the truth of our lives. That is the path to real growth.

Someone recently suggested to me that the spiritual journey is like a moving sidewalk. We move along on it whether we do anything or not. Others believe that we have to do all the work and then God will reward us with spiritual growth. Perhaps the truth is somewhere in the middle. We are called to grow in the light of God's love for us. Our desire to grow in goodness is our response to the grace of God already moving through us. God is the one who has begun this love relationship. Our response to God is just that—a response. We will grow and blossom just by loving God back. That is really what spiritual growth and holiness are all about.

As in a garden, different gifts blossom within us at different times in our lives. In some seasons we grow roses while in others we grow tomatoes. Neither is good or bad. Each has a place in our lives. For surely, "There is an appointed time for everything . . ." (Eccl. 3:1).

An array of sunflowers once taught me an important truth about outer and inner gardens. Early one morning I drove past a field of sunflowers as I was traveling to eastern Long Island. They were all facing east, looking at the sun. Late that afternoon I passed the same field on my way home. All the flowers were facing west. I wonder if anyone saw them turn. They had followed the source of the light throughout the day. Can you imagine how we would grow if we followed the source of Light throughout our day?

Sometimes we need to work on our garden so that it will flower. Maybe some cutting back or pruning is in order. We may even need to do some transplanting of our ideas and expectations to experience the mystery of growth. Clinging to ideas about how we ought to be can block the gateway to mystery. Honoring what is true for us in the present moment puts us in touch with glory—God's face reflected within us. And God longs for us to grow and flower.

St. Paul tells us of God's longing in a most powerful way. "If God is for us, who can be against us?" (Rom. 8:31). As we journey through the day, isn't it reassuring to know that God is for us? If the "soil" of our inner garden is God's love and support, does it really matter who is against us? No one's power can destroy what God is bringing to life in us.

Our growth cannot just be left to God. Our inner gardens need our touch. We need to enrich our lives with compassion, understanding, and courage. The actual work of gardening is a wonderful metaphor for tending our souls. Our spiritual life, like a garden, does not need constant attention; but it does need continual attention. The soil in a garden needs to be turned and aerated to give forth its treasure. We, too, hold a treasure; and that treasure needs our attention so that it may be unearthed.

To garden effectively, we need tools to turn the earth, plant bulbs, and prune them for growth. Tools are also important for inner gardening. Attitudes and actions are tools that help us move our souls and honor our own truth so that we may grow and blossom into fullness. There are several tools that I suggest you use for your inner gardening.

The tool of listening. I recently saw a greeting card that had the following sentiment printed on the front cover: "We all need a good listening." What a marvelous truth! When we really listen to someone, we give that person a priceless gift. Listening is uninterrupted presence to another. This gift affirms the other person and shows that we cherish them.

The tool of affection. Be generous with your kindness. Reach out and embrace someone who is hurting. We can become so fearful of exposing ourselves to rejection that we hold back our feelings. After a while, we become detached from our feelings altogether. We may even forget that we can feel. Remember, you have to dig in the dirt to plant. We all need to get a little messy once in awhile. Let yourself feel.

The tool of laughter. When was the last time you had a good belly laugh? Our society seems to have relegated breaking into hysterics to children. Often even they are chastised for their outbursts of joy. I went to a very funny movie a few weeks ago. It was so funny that I was laughing out loud. The people sitting around me turned to look at me as if I had lost my mind. And this was a comedy! I continued to enjoy the movie; but for personal safety, I buried my laughter in my coat, which was folded on my lap. I suggest you find a safe place and laugh yourself silly. Believe me, you will experience a great freedom.

The tool of compliments. Why do so many of us have trouble accepting a compliment? Any time I compliment a friend of mine on her clothing, she immediately tells me she got it on sale. I want to tell her that although I love a sale, I believe she is worth full price.

I suggest that you take a few minutes to look in your mirror. Instead of voicing the usual criticisms, try saying, "You are still here and you are doing fine." We have already received the greatest compliment—God is on our side. That is truly reason to celebrate. Try letting the gift of a compliment wash over you and fill your heart with joy.

My neighbor has an extensive English cottage garden in her backyard. It is quite beautiful. Our garden, on the other hand, has a few irises, some black-eyed Susans, and two Montauk daisy bushes. It may not rival a botanical garden, but it is ours and we love it. The size of the garden is not what matters. How we tend it is what makes it our own. We, too, are all different; but each of us is God's own. I once saw a wall plaque that aptly captures this thought. It said, "God loves each of us as though we were the only one."

The sunflower grows toward the light. I encourage you to keep moving toward the light of God's love in your life. You will be amazed at how you will grow.

Sister Pat

Soul Suggestions

Week One

Do you know someone who needs a good listening to? Why not offer them the gift of your presence this week?

Week Two

Write a letter to God in which you pour out your heart. Be honest about your hopes, dreams, failures, and concerns. Let this letter be your prayer. Remember, God is for you!

Week Three

Rent a funny video, invite a friend to watch it with you, and laugh yourself silly. (Don't forget the popcorn!)

Week Four

Each day this week give yourself a compliment whenever you look in the mirror.

August

GRATITUDE: A PLACE IN THE HEART

Dear Woman of Soul:

Has your heart ever been warmed or broken by someone or something? When this happens, we can actually feel the emotion deep within. Even the Scriptures speak of this in Luke 2:19, "And Mary kept all these things, reflecting on them in her heart." The great mystery of the heart is that it is so much more than a physical pump. Not only does it keep us alive physiologically, it also enlivens us emotionally and spiritually.

A number of years ago the movie *Places in the Heart* was released. Sally Fields received an Academy Award for her magnificent portrayal of the many facets of a woman's emotional life. Although I enjoyed the movie, the title is what resounds within me. There are many places in our hearts: places of warm memories, places of laughter, places of tears, places of hurt, and places of forgiveness, to name a few.

We are now in the hot and hazy days of late summer. Hopefully you have enjoyed some time of extended vacation and relaxation. The slower pace of the month of August gives us an opportunity to use some of our free time to reflect on our journey. I suggest that you take time to look at the places in your heart before the pace picks up again. Walk through your memories with God as your companion. When you get to the place of gratitude, rest there for a while. For this is the place that gives hope and encouragement for all that is to come.

There are many definitions for the word gratitude, but the meaning of this great emotion is much deeper than any definition. It can be said that gratitude is the response of the heart to all that is given. In gratitude we are moved to thankfulness for all of life's gifts, especially the simple, the ordinary, and those things we have come to expect. I call these the "given." Gratitude, a response to the "given," which is freely bestowed on us, warms our hearts with thankfulness.

When I hear "the given," I am reminded of the phrase we often hear, "Well, that is a given." We seem to dismiss someone or something with this expression. But let's think for a minute about "the givens" in our lives: a child saying thank you for your attention, a stranger's kindness, the faithfulness of a loved one. These are all responses we may expect in our lives. We may even see them as "the givens," but they are so much more.

After my auto accident, going to the hospital for surgeries almost became "a given" in my life. Nobody was surprised by my hospitalizations because they had become a common occurrence. Yet each one was a difficult and painful experience for me. To change the atmosphere of surgery as "a given" in my life, Michele began to give me hospital gifts. "Just think of it as an occasion for a gift," she told me. That certainly changed my attitude. It also made others aware that each of these occasions was unique and often difficult. Of course, some of my family and friends began to complain when I announced that I was going to the hospital and expected a gift. Spoil sports that they are!

The other day I was driving with a friend and we were trying to merge into a heavily traveled road. My friend said, "It's a given that sooner or later someone will let us in." We waited eight minutes! When "the given" finally happened, I was very grateful. I even blew kisses to the driver who yielded, to thank her for her kindness. Maybe "the givens" should not be taken so lightly. They may be occasions for blowing kisses.

When I was celebrating my twenty-fifth anniversary as a Dominican, we had planned a celebration on the East End of Long Island. The location was beautiful and most of those invited responded that they would be attending. The day of the event we had a Nor'easter accompanied by high winds and a deluge of rain. Many of the guests had to travel a long distance, and I was upset that they would be unable to come because of the storm. My friend reassured me that since they had responded that they were coming, I should expect that they would come. She was telling me it was a "given" that the guests would weather the storm to be there. I, on the other hand, was overwhelmed with gratitude to see over one hundred people who drove through floods and around downed trees and power lines to be present. At that moment the words of the poet, e.e. cummings, came to mind. "The eyes of my eyes were opened." Wouldn't it be wonderful if the eyes of our eyes were opened to all "the givens"?

My greatest surprise is that there are "givens" in our lives. After all, everything, even the smallest kindness, is a gift. And all gifts have their home in God's love. So much of what we consider "given" is a gift from God. What would exist if it weren't for

God's love? God did not have to create anyone or anything. All is gift! When we allow ourselves to be surprised by God's "givens," we will be surprised again and again. We will surely live in wonder.

I invite you to set up a lawn chair in your outer and inner gardens and spend some time reflecting on the giftedness of "the givens" in your life. To help you with this process, I am suggesting three attitudes that may assist you in opening the "eyes of your eyes."

Do not take anyone or anything for granted. Have you noticed that the prayers of children are almost always those of gratitude? A woman I know shared with me a wonderful experience of her daughter's prayer. They were taking a walk and came upon a beautiful wildflower. The little girl wanted to pick the flower. Her mother suggested that they leave it there so others could enjoy its beauty as a gift from God. Just as they were ready to continue their walk, the little girl said aloud, "Thanks for the pretty flower, God." Simple, yet profound, this prayer sums up a quality we are all called to develop or renew in our lives.

Something seems to happen as we grow older. The newness and freshness of life wears off, and we have a tendency to focus on what we don't have, what's missing, what our problems and struggles are. What has happened to the wonder? Recognizing the place of gratitude in our hearts calls us to wake up. And the minute we are awake, we stop taking people and things for granted.

Learn to be a gracious receiver. We have probably all heard the expression: "It is more blessed to give than to receive." Well, I simply do not believe that! I think we would all be a lot more blessed if we allowed ourselves to accept the graciousness of others. I am sure you know people that just cannot receive a gift without giving you a bigger and better gift in return. My aunt lived by this principle. She was very generous and gave us all lovely gifts. She, however, never wanted any gifts and appeared to be embarrassed by them.

Thus began the saga of the bedspread! I decided one Christmas that I was going to give her a gift she would really like. I wanted her to know she was loved and could be happy to receive a gift. This was my first mistake. The second mistake was to start buying bedspreads! I ordered the first spread through a catalog. When it arrived, I could see that it just would not do. Off I went to the store's catalog desk to return it. This was no small feat, as I was using crutches to get around. I dragged the huge box through the store with a luggage carrier. While there, I ordered a second bedspread. I then saw a beautiful spread in another shop. You see, I was determined to buy something she would just love. (Have you ever been on one of these insane journeys?) Of course, I bought the third spread. When the second spread arrived in the mail, I had to get out the luggage carrier again to return another large box to the catalog desk at the store.

I really wanted to please my aunt. Was she pleased? I have no idea. She was clearly overwhelmed by the size of the gift box and simply mumbled something indiscernible. What I do know is that for several months afterward I received unexpected gifts from her. My aunt died recently. As I was gathering together her things, I found a large box in the back of her closet containing the unopened spread!

The bedspread insanity was my attempt to have my aunt experience the joy of receiving a gift that was lovely and carried love. Looking back on the situation, I realize I should have accepted her as she was. I am not responsible for changing anyone but myself. My attitude about receiving is what I must work on. I suggest you work on this in your life situation, too. Maybe today it would be both a discipline and a joy to just accept the graciousness of another without feeling we must repay it with something bigger and better.

Be a blessing. I think in order to be a blessing we have to acknowledge blessings that we have received. When was a moment that you felt blessed? Why not spend some time just giving thanks for the gift?

Sometime ago I asked a group of women to write about a moment in their lives when they felt they were one with everything. Some call this a peak experience. The responses of these women were overwhelming. Many of them thanked me for giving them the opportunity to recall such blessings in their lives. When we can remember being blessed, the grace of blessing begins to flow within us. To bless is to see and acknowledge the goodness of another. God breathes life into us, and we breathe out blessing. Someone loves us, and we in turn are more lovable. This is how blessing becomes a way of life.

Of course, being a blessing means being awake, truly alive and breathing. Sadly, many of us are not truly alive. We seem to sip at life. If we just sip at the air, we will not have much life within us. If we just sip at the grace God breathes into us, we will be weak and unable to breathe out many blessings. To be a person of gratitude, we must wake up to life and blessing.

There are many places in our hearts. As you leave your lawn chair, I ask you to take with you "the eyes of your eyes," opened and thankful for the gifts of all "the givens" in your life.

Soul Suggestions

Week One

Write down the "the givens" in your life. Take your time doing this, perhaps even setting it aside for a time and then coming back to it. Pick one and throw kisses at it this week.

Week Two

You are invited to take time and write "the givens" from God in your life. (Some of these may overlap with last week's.) Light a candle in your house each day during this week as a reminder to be grateful for the light of God's love.

Week Three

Open the eyes of your eyes and see someone who is performing a task that makes your life easier. It may be someone you don't know—the food store employee who surprises you by packing your groceries, the lawn care person, or the maid who cleans your hotel room. The list is endless! Thank the person with a small gift.

Week Four

Each day set aside ten minutes to deeply breathe in your blessings.

September

AND YOUR SOUL SHALL DANCE

Dear Woman of Soul:

"I've got rhythm, I've got music . . . who could ask for anything more?" This catchy little tune has been playing in my mind for the past several weeks. After a hot and humid August, when people seemed to be dragging themselves around looking for the next respite from air conditioning, September offers us a new step. It is as if a different tune is playing in the universe. I can see it in the way people walk. No longer burdened by heat and humidity, they appear to have a new freedom that shows itself in a lively, rhythmic gait.

My observations as a confirmed people watcher stirred up in me a wonderful memory. Several years ago I was attending a family celebration at my brother Jim's house. Against a background of soft rock music, the adults were talking while the children gathered around a new play gym. Off to one side of the backyard my niece Olivia, then about 2 years old, was playing by herself. She was dancing to the music with her little doll. Her steps had a delightful repetition, and I thought to myself, "How did she learn that?" Of course, she hadn't learned it at all. Her rhythm came from inside. She was born with it. We are all born with an inner rhythm. We don't need to learn the dance of life. We just need to get in touch with our own rhythm and the dance will begin.

I would like to share some reflections with you on what I see as two different dances we do in life. The first is the dance of the expected. Its rhythm has a familiar beat of phrases like "you can't do that," "you should have known better," and "because you have to." Statements like these restrain and often paralyze our steps, robbing us of our natural rhythm. No longer experiencing the freedom of little Olivia, we find ourselves imprisoned by expectations.

I have a marionette in my room. Her name is Tallulah, honoring a term of affection my father called me by as a child. Tallulah has four strings, each attached to one of her arms or legs. When I pick her up, she stands tall until I begin to pull the strings. With each tug of a string, Tallulah awkwardly moves under my direction. The dance of the expected is very much like this. When we are consumed by the desire to please others and fulfill their expectations of us, our movements become awkward and out of sync with our natural rhythm.

Can you imagine if we began to count the strings attached to our lives? Let's consider four of them right now. The first three strings, *should*, *have to*, and *can't*, are common in the lives of many women. Many of us have heard these words so often since early childhood that they have taken up residence within us. The last string you can name from your own experience.

We have become more the recipients than the authors of our lives. Because we have come to believe these words, we no longer need outside voices to "pull our strings." We do it ourselves. Just think about the way you talk to yourself when you look in the mirror. If most of us spoke to our houseplants the way we speak to ourselves, they would wither up and die! Phrases like "I should have" and "I can't" limit us and break our inner rhythm.

There are steps in the dance of life; natural patterns that help us live joyfully. Strings distort those patterns. They pull, jerk, and hold us back from who we can be. When we break the rhythm of our lives, we become clumsy and awkward within ourselves. How often have you heard someone say, "I feel out of sorts?" "Out of sorts" is a good description for someone who is bound by strings.

When someone else's expectations of how we should be and act are added to our own, our movement becomes even more restrained. We find ourselves dancing to a rhythm that is not our own. We are out of sync with our soul and, therefore, with ourselves. A woman recently related a story to me that powerfully illustrates this point. She had remarried and her husband was having an increasingly difficult time getting along with her eighteen-year-old son. One evening as the couple was preparing to go to their square dance class, an argument erupted between her husband and her son. The husband put her son out of the house and told him not to come back. He then angrily insisted they still go to the class. Shortly after they arrived, the woman told her husband she wanted to leave. She said, "My feet just don't want to dance tonight." We need to be true to our inner rhythm; we need to be in sync with our souls to truly dance in life.

All of creation is in rhythm. The robins return in springtime, the tides ebb and flow, and flowers bloom in their season. A few weeks ago I experienced a rare moment in the universe's rhythm.

After the sun had set, the sky was still lit. I saw a reddish glow forming a stripe across the sky as far as I could see. I later discovered that it was a reflection of the northern lights reaching all the way down to Long Island. The universe dances rhythmically and in color, too!

The dance of freedom, the second dance we do, also has a natural pattern. My niece Olivia's dance had repetitive steps. Of course, there was a little twist and dip here and there, but there was definitely a pattern. We need to have a plan in life, but the plan cannot have us. There needs to be space to improvise in situations. Having a sense of order is important, but it should never be at the expense of moments of spontaneity. Life does have a natural flow. Going with the flow may be the greatest gift of freedom we can give ourselves.

Some people truly enjoy being miserable. I am sure you know people who can whine about anything; but they are the exception. Most of us want to have attitudes that encourage a sense of freedom. We are the ones who will cut the strings!

I'd like to share with you some attitudes that I believe counter *should, can't,* and *have to.* They are *choose it, want it* and *will it.* Even if at some point in your life you had instilled in you the idea that there are many things you have to do, even more things you should do, and of course, so many things you can't do; you can change. It's all about attitude. Our choices direct our lives. Often we make choices without considering the consequences. A friend of mine enrolled her daughter in gymnastics. That choice led to her rising at 4:30 a.m. and traveling many hours to go to meets. She was seldom able to attend her other children's concerts and field trips. She felt burdened and guilty; but she did not want to go back on her word to her daughter. My friend began to feel overwhelmed by a long list of shoulds. The initial choice was not a good one in the context of her life. After some discussion, her daughter agreed to go to dance school instead.

Good choices promote a positive attitude. There are many things that I feel I have to do, but the *have to* is born out of my choice. Making a commitment is quite different from having an expectation. Because I want the essence of the commitment, I will freely do what needs to be done to achieve it. What do you really want? When you can answer that question, your life will take on a different sense of order. Because you want something, you will it. You make choices to move in a certain direction. When you will it, you put things into motion. Then your choices and not someone else's expectations motivate you. Not everything you do will be enjoyable, but you will be on the path to what you desire.

Several years ago my friend Michele found a wonderful house hidden in the woods. It was a magical place that had been abandoned for years. We discovered that the house was in the process of foreclosure and would be auctioned off. Michele and I made a commitment to secure it for her. The first thing she did was to put a note on her bathroom mirror that said she was the proud owner of the house. The notes multiplied until wherever she went, one would catch her eye.

Through job changes, car break downs and my automobile accident, we followed the progress of the house. She even went to the bank to be pre-approved for a mortgage. What a proud day it was when I accompanied Michele to town hall and watched her successfully bid on the house. Not all the steps between finding the house and obtaining it were convenient or enjoyable. Many times we were stressed by the number of phone calls, paper work, and deadlines. These activities were not a burden, though, because they were part of the greater choice. She wanted the house, she got it, and to this day she lives in that house hidden in the woods.

When you are the author of your own life, the burdens of your choices are part of the joy of your decisions. Joseph Campbell, the renowned anthropologist, felt strongly that each of us should follow our bliss. "If you follow your bliss . . . you put yourself on a kind of track that has been there all the while . . . waiting for you, the life you ought to be living. Wherever you are, if you are following your bliss . . . you are enjoying that refreshment, that life within you, all the time . . ." The prophet Zephaniah tells us in 3:17 "Our God will dance with shouts of joy for us." Let your soul dance and feel God's pleasure. This is the dance of freedom. This is your life, your bliss: you *choose it*, you *want it*, and you *will it*.

Just take a moment to fill in the following: "If I gave myself permission to follow my dreams, I would _____." Is this worth your commitment? If your answer is "Yes," then you have found the steps to your dance.

I would like to leave you with a wonderful thought from the movie *Chariots of Fire*. Asked about his running, the lead character said, "When I run, I feel God's pleasure." I know we will all feel God's pleasure when we become the authors of our own lives.

Sister Pat

Soul Suggestions

Week One

You are invited to make your strings visible. Cut four pieces of twine, each about 12 inches long, and place them on the table in front of you. Identify some of the strings pulling at your life and label each of these strings accordingly. Each week hang one string in a place easily visible to you. Ask yourself what you need to be able to cut the string and how you will get what you need to do it.

Week Two

Take ten minutes each morning this week to sit quietly and listen to the rhythm of your body and soul. Hear your heartbeat and feel your breath move through you. Can you identify your rhythm? Give thanks for the life force within you and for all of creation.

Week Three

Reflect on the thought: "If I gave myself permission to follow my dream, I would. . . ." This week begin to put in place what you need to do in order to achieve this dream.

Week Four

Did you cut the strings yet? Is now a good time? Take a long walk or go running, mindful of moving in your own rhythm. Allow yourself to feel God's pleasure.

October

WITH HEARTS AFIRE

Dear Woman of Soul:

My backyard was ablaze and I stood in wonder and awe. It was as if some divine being had flitted around my yard in an organized frenzy dropping color everywhere. Although this idea appealed to my imagination, I decided to research this annual magical mystery. I discovered that the colors in the leaves do not come from the outside. They are within the leaves all along, just waiting to burst forth when the right atmospheric conditions are present.

We share so much with nature. The "fire" I witnessed in my backyard reminds me of a wonderful Gospel story in Luke 24. This story is about two disciples who left Jerusalem and were traveling to Emmaus after Jesus died on the cross and his followers dispersed or went into hiding. During their journey of several miles, they got into a heated conversation about the loss of their hopes and dreams. Their words "we had hoped" show that hope was no longer a traveling companion for them. They were walking away from Jerusalem, the city of promise.

In the midst of their sad discussion, Jesus approached them. The two were so caught up in their own distress that they did not recognize him. Jesus asked them what they were talking about, and they told him about the tragedy that had taken place in

Jerusalem. As the three traveled along, Jesus explained how the Scriptures foretold the events of the previous days. His companions were enraptured by Jesus' words. When they reached their destination, they invited him to stay with them. During dinner Jesus took bread, blessed it, and shared it with them. In that moment their eyes were opened and they knew their Lord was present among them. Then Jesus disappeared.

Left in this "God-moment," the two began to discuss what they had just experienced. Trying to capture the feeling of being with Jesus, one said, "Were not our hearts burning within us?" I love this image because it so aptly captures their sacred encounter. Something happened in their time with Jesus that touched them and set their hearts on fire. Their passion was rekindled and they left the safety of the inn to venture out on the dangerous road back to Jerusalem, the place of promise. Their concern for personal safety was overcome by their desire to share what had set their hearts on fire. They returned to the disheartened community of believers to announce, "We have seen the Lord!"

Amazingly, personal safety loses its usual primary importance in the face of passion. Set on fire, we can do things we never dreamed possible. After all, what is life if there is nothing to die for? Or maybe even more importantly, what is life if there is nothing to LIVE for?

This passion, this fire, is what sets our lives ablaze in brilliant colors. To be truly understood, this passion, which involves intense emotion and energy, must be experienced. While words fail to capture it, you will recognize its presence when you are being driven forward by it. Please take a moment now to reflect on two questions. What sets your heart on fire? What is at the heart of your fire? If life situations have been "putting out your fire" you may need more time to remember. Don't worry—the embers of our passion can never be extinguished. They are the sparks of the divine within each of us.

I thought long and hard about how to explain this passion that resides within each of us. I believe the fire cannot be taught—it must be caught. So, using Jesus' method of storytelling, I would like to share three parables, which I believe explain how I have caught the fire. Perhaps they will help to fan the embers of your soul.

I call the first parable "The Woman Who Embraced Life and Saw Faces in the Floor." When I was a young girl, we got a new kitchen floor. It had a blue-gray pattern of diamonds with what appeared to be clouds in the center of each diamond. My mother insisted that if you looked closely enough you could see faces in those clouds. My father came home one evening to find his wife and three children sitting on the floor staring at the clouds. We saw those faces! Imagination is the spark that ignites the fire.

My mother gifted me with a sense of possibility at a young age. She always saw through a situation to what could be. In her wisdom she encouraged me to be and do anything I wanted in life and not to let the fact that I was a girl hold me back. This was quite revolutionary in the 1950's. My mother not only gave life to my brothers and me, but also "lifed" us to all that was possible. That was some way to start a fire!

I call the second parable "The Man You Could Believe In and The Christmas Trees." By the rest of my family's standards, my father was a quiet man. That's not to say he was withdrawn. My family can be very noisy! He was a simple man who worked very hard and wanted only the best for his family. I felt very safe with my Dad and have come to realize what a great gift that was. His integrity was a powerful force in our home. When he said he was going to do something, he did it. Integrity is a great fire-stoker.

The Christmas season would begin for us with a pilgrimage to get our Christmas tree. Unlike many families who travel to a Christmas tree farm to cut down their tree, we went to the docks on the west side of Manhattan (I was definitely a city kid!). As was our custom, we would buy a bundle of trees. We would then pick one for ourselves and my father would give the others to families who could not afford a tree. One Christmas, however, we kept two trees. One had a beautiful top and the other had a beautiful bottom. My father cut them in half and connected the better halves with a pipe. We had some tree! Creativity brightens the fire.

I entitled the third parable "The Woman Who Saw Beyond Her Time and Laughed." Thirty-five years ago religious life was undergoing many changes and we struggled to discern the way of truth. I was privileged to meet an elderly sister who became both friend and mentor to me. Mother Adelaide was a great source of wisdom for me. Our sixty-three year age difference made no difference at all. She loved me for who I was and for who I could become. Of all the treasures she gave me, the greatest was her nurturing of my budding love for God and my desire to preach His Word. Mother Adelaide's sense of history helped to ground me in the Dominican traditions and gave me wings to fly into the future, no matter what it held. Vision and trust fan the fire.

What is the fire in your heart? What is at the heart of your fire? Whom did you catch the fire from? Who has kindled the fire within you? We all know people who believe

I once had a conversation with a very old and holy sister. I asked her how you become truly holy. She replied that Jesus came to set the world on fire, but sadly, most of us do not jump in. Rather, we stand around and warm our hands by the fire. What a great meditation that could be!

A story I once heard might be a good way to illuminate this thought. Many years ago a young spiritual seeker went to live in a far-off community of hermits. One day she approached the community elder with a perplexing question. After spending time in the community, she wondered why the people arrived with great fervor but then some lost heart and left while others stayed. The elder responded, "Let me tell you a story."

"One day my old dog and I were sitting outside my hut when a great big rabbit ran right by us. My dog jumped up and began chasing that rabbit. His barking and yelping attracted other dogs in the area, and soon they were all in hot pursuit of the rabbit. Over the hills and down the creek they went. This continued all morning. During the afternoon the dogs dropped out of the chase one by one. Only my dog stayed on the trail of that rabbit. The story contains the answer to your question."

"Quite confused, the young seeker inquired, 'How is a rabbit chase like the pursuit of holiness?' 'Oh,' he replied, 'you are asking the wrong question. The correct question is 'Why did my dog continue when all the others gave up?' The answer is that only my dog saw the rabbit and was ablaze with passion. When you do not see the rabbit, you lose your fervor for the chase.' "

Much like the dog with the rabbit, our personal experience of God enlivens our passion for the journey. We can take others' word for the grandeur of God, but that will not set us on fire. I believe we can catch the imagination, integrity, creativity, vision, and trust from those who are afire. When we put ourselves in the right atmosphere, we will have the courage to jump into the fire of God. My hope and prayer for you, my sisters, is that you may see and that you may burn brightly in many colors.

Happy Autumn!

Sister Pat

Soul Suggestions

During the first three weeks of this month, I ask you to allow the following questions to stay deep within you. Let them be your companions throughout the day

Week One

What is life if there is nothing to die for? What is life if there is nothing to live for?

Week Two

What sets your heart on fire? What is the heart of your fire?

Week Three

Whom did you catch the fire from? Who has kindled and nurtured the fire within you?

Week Four

Pass the fire on. Be imaginative in sharing your fire with someone.

November

THANK GOD I'M ENOUGH

Dear Woman of Soul:

Well, we are about to do it again, or if we are among the lucky ones, another female family member is doing it this year. Yes, I am talking about the Thanksgiving feast! There is something very important about this spectacular ritual. It speaks of family and tradition. And yet in the midst of the hoped-for Walton experience, there is often anxiety, dis-ease, and too often the questions: "Was I good enough?" and "Did I do enough?"

All of this may have something to do with the standards of ritual set by Martha Stewart and other divas of lifestyle; however, I believe something else is responsible. How many of us only feel good about ourselves when we have made others happy? To be kind and considerate of others' feelings and wishes is a laudable gift. But, when it becomes the way we define ourselves, we have a problem. I call this the "enough syndrome." You can tell if you suffer from this soul-debilitating disease if you find yourself using the "enough language."

I am amazed at how often I hear the word "enough" uttered in the form of a personal deficit. Haven't we all said, "I am not organized enough," or "I am not pretty enough, " or "I didn't do enough for them," or perhaps most often, "I am not thin enough?" These expressions of self-deficiency keep drawing us down to a place where we feel inadequate and insignificant.

What do we as women measure ourselves against? Do we have built in yardsticks by which we frequently grade ourselves inch by inch? When we do this, we buy into a mentality that we most probably would not believe if we are in our right minds!

What is happening when we find ourselves in the "enough quandary?" I believe the answer has something to do with what and who we refer to when looking at and evaluating ourselves. Psychologists explain this as a choice for object-referral in our lives. Object-referral is measuring ourselves against an object, title, man, friend, or child. Anything outside of ourselves can become an object or point of reference for how we judge ourselves. The mirror, mirror on the wall seems to be continually telling us that because of our personal lacking in some area of our lives, we are not the fairest of them all. This frequently occurs with mothers of adult children who hold themselves responsible for the actions of their children. Their "enough" statements may sound like "What should I have done differently?" or "If only I had. . . ." This line of thinking can cause an inner sense of uncertainty and dis-ease that eventually expresses itself in physical and emotional disease.

Many years ago when I entered the Dominican Order, I stepped into a new world that constituted marvelous traditions. I was told a moving story on my first day in the convent while being given a tour of the complex that included a century-old chapel. High above an altar on the left side of the chapel was a mural of Jesus and St. Dominic. As the story goes, St. Dominic had a dream about heaven, and much to his surprise, he did not see one Dominican in heaven. Dominic was greatly saddened and asked Jesus where all his followers had gone. Jesus then brought Dominic to Mary, the Mother of Jesus. Mary opened her magnificent blue mantle and there, under her mantle, were all the Dominicans. I was wonderstruck by the story! Through it I came to see how special Dominicans were to Jesus and Mary. We were so special that Mary held us close to herself and protected us. This story was a source of peace and hope for me throughout the years. One day, however, it all changed.

About ten years ago I took a ride with a friend who is a Franciscan priest. We went to visit the seminary where he studied for the priesthood. During a tour of the building we entered an old chapel. It was rather dark, with soft rays of light from the sun streaming through the windows. My friend was anxious to show me something that was very close to his heart. Yes, it was a mural; but this time St. Francis was standing with Jesus before Mary, whose mantle was held wide open. Guess who was standing under her mantle? Franciscans, of course! My heart sank as my friend related his story. It seems that the first day he was in the seminary they were taken on a tour. When they arrived at the chapel, they were told that St. Francis had a dream about heaven and did not see any Franciscans. The Franciscans had been telling the same story!

I came away from that visit feeling a sense of loss about how special Dominicans are to God. Later, after some reflection, my eyes were opened to a new reality. We are all very special to God! As a matter of fact, YOU are that special. The prophet Isaiah gives us a wonderful image of just how special each of us is to God. He tells us in Isaiah 62 that we are each unique and a rare jewel in the diadem of God. Imagine that perhaps you are a glistening emerald or a luminous ruby in God's crown. This image shows us that we are "enough" exactly as we are—enough for God. I believe this knowledge is reason for us to rejoice. To be enough, we have only to be ourselves, our true selves, not the selves we have invented to meet others' expectations or to compensate for our harsh self-judgments.

The opposite of object-referral is self-referral. With self-referral we measure ourselves from our own centers. The measure is not outward, but rather, inward, on a path that does not include rulers, inches, or performances. Self-referral has to do with finding who we are. Thomas Merton, a modern-day mystic, often told his audiences that when you come to your true center, there you would find God. This journey is one of truth, accepting our limitations and uncovering our gifts. It is truly a path of prayer, in which the traveler does not so much say prayers as live prayer in close companionship with God. Self-referral then becomes a reflection of our lives in communion with our God, who sees us as a rare jewel.

Self-referral is a process of thinking. We must throw off the heavy cloak of negative thinking, under which we are never enough. We must stop putting ourselves down and letting old voices of criticism that told us we were stupid, ugly, or useless freeze us in place.

Right thinking does not happen overnight. We need to develop practices in our interior life that give space for new and positive thoughts to grow. I suggest three practices that help to prepare the soil of our souls for the seeds of right thinking.

The first practice is of silence. In this information age, we are bombarded with noise, images, and chatter. Imagine taking one hour of silence each day. If that is a little too frightening, how about taking one half-hour a day to begin. This means no TV, music, or phone calls. Quiet time is an opportunity for the mind to divest itself of all the unnecessary "stuff" that is stored inside us. At first you might find your mind running wild. I liken this to a closet that has been overloaded with coats, boots, toys, and junk. When the door is opened, all the stuff comes tumbling out. Only after it has landed at our feet can we sort through the mess.

Our minds need to be emptied of all the negative thoughts that have been crammed into them. After our thoughts have tumbled out and landed at our feet, we can begin to sort out and discard those we do not want or need. A time of silence is an emptying. When we are not filling our minds, we are giving them an opportunity to be emptied. A half-hour to an hour a day of silence can provide you with a wonderful time for inner housecleaning.

Second, we have the practice of the present moment. In medieval monasteries young monks were often encouraged to spend some time each day being present to what they were doing. This may sound simple; yet it is the key to true contemplation. I would suggest that for ten minutes you try to be present to what you are doing. Simply put, when you are doing the dishes, be present to the dishes. You should not be thinking about what you will do next or rehashing the previous day. Be present to the dishes! This practice can also be used in any of your daily life activities. The discipline is to be present to whatever you are doing or the person you are with. Believe me, this is no small undertaking, but it is the beginning of centering yourself. The journey to the center is one of paying attention to the present.

The third practice is to be non-judgmental. Can you imagine going through the day without criticizing someone else or yourself? So many of us seem to have an invisible ruler by which we measure others and ourselves against a set of rules that have been engraved in our minds. Often these rules of life are not truly our own; in fact, if we gave them serious, quiet thought, we would probably discard many of them. Yet, somehow they continue to be a standard by which we judge and are judged.

This kind of negative thinking keeps us from growing and living the full life that God longs to give us. We are called to grow into an awareness of our world and ourselves that is both compassionate and gracious. This is seeing with the eyes of God. Sadly, however, too many of us only feel good about ourselves when we are putting someone else down. In reality, when we judge others, we are belittling ourselves by pouring out the beauty within us. When we are encrusted in bitterness, we have difficulty seeing ourselves as a gem in the royal diadem.

Silence of the heart, attentiveness to the present moment, and a nonjudgmental spirit soften our hearts and polish the gem within. Wouldn't it be wonderful to walk through the day with compassion and gentleness? These are the gifts of a woman who knows deep in her soul that she is enough. After all, God has told her so!

For many years I was stuck in a place between "I'm good enough" and "I'm not good enough" as I labored over

Thanksgiving meals for family and friends. I made sure every-thing was perfect, from the place settings to the gravy boat that had a tea light candle for the relative who always asked, "Is the gravy hot?"

After my serious car accident, I found myself bedridden for the Thanksgiving feast preparation and knew that a break in tradition was in order. That year we ate a catered meal off paper plates. One concerned friend, with a nod to my compulsion, made sure that all the turkeys on the paper plates were facing in the same direc-tion! Seeing this guy aligning turkeys, when he ordinarily would not even notice that there were plates on the table, made me real-ize just how crazy I can be!

Believe it or not, we had Thanksgiving without me playing retriever—running to the kitchen for extra spoons and needed utensils. Surprisingly, turkey and stuffing do not need to be served on china to taste delicious and washing mounds of pots and pans is not the perfect ending to a perfect day after all!

Actually, when you think about it, Thanksgiving is the glorious feast of "enough." We gather to give thanks to God for all that we have, and that truly is enough. The real meaning of Thanksgiving stands as an antidote to all women who suffer from the "enough syndrome." At Thanksgiving we are called to recognize and be grateful for all that we are in addition to all that we have. To be thankful, we must believe that we are royal gems who are blessed by God.

Take a deep breath, remember the blessings, and give thanks for you. This is a good start to the celebration of Thanksgiving.

Sister Pat

Soul Suggestions

Week One

Gather pictures of people or things that you measure yourself by. Place the pictures on your refrigerator. Each morning pick one picture to carry with you throughout the day.

Week Two

Use this week to revisit the gift of silence you uncovered earlier this year. Has the practice of silence become a part of your life? This is an opportunity to reclaim your inner peace.

Week Three

The practice of the present moment is the way of prayer. As you are preparing for the Thanksgiving celebration, be mindful of the people who grew, tended, and harvested your bounty. Also, be present to those with whom you will share the feast and those for whom there will be no feast.

Week Four

This week companion yourself in truth. Rather than judging yourself for who you are not, cherish yourself for who you are. Let the feast begin!

December

WAITING FOR THE LIGHT

Dear Woman of Soul:

I am in South Florida to attend a conference entitled: "The Adventure of Being Alive." I could not resist the draw of the title and to hear one of the speakers, who wrote a book that I am crazy about. Overall, the quality of the speakers has been poor and the schedule has been grueling. Let's remember, though, that it is early December and I am in Florida. So, there is very little to complain about!

Last night I spent some time reflecting on the conference title, "The Adventure of Being Alive." Helen Keller once said, "Life is a daring adventure or nothing at all." This can be hard to believe when the dark and cold of winter descend; and it can become a distant memory when the car breaks down, you are late for work or an appointment, a family member is ill, and you still haven't started your Christmas shopping. How quickly the adventure can become the catastrophe of being alive!

One of the conference speakers asked the question, "What sustains you in the darkness?" I find this question to be both poignant and funny. This past summer Michele and I had a section of our house painted. The painter suggested we take down the outdated track lighting in the kitchen. The idea sounded good at the time. I was not aware of the "odyssey of darkness" that was to follow.

Our kitchen ceiling has a sixteen-foot peak. We had to search for a fixture that would provide enough light for the distance from ceiling to floor. We didn't give this much thought during the sunny days of August. When September came, the subject of a kitchen light began to emerge in our conversations. A pilgrimage to the "shrine" of Home Depot gave us some ideas and the frightful reality of prices.

In October we moved a bedroom lamp onto the kitchen counter, donned the reading glasses and hoped for the best. (It's a good thing I am not Julia Childs!) Visits to the kitchen became a trust walk, as the sun rested on the horizon at 5 p.m. in late October.

The major domo of our estate (otherwise known as the handyman) arrived bright and early on November 1 to install the fixture. After careful inspection of the situation he informed us that the fixture was too heavy for him to both hold and drill into the ceiling at the same time. We would have to wait until he could get help. After paying for his time, we were still in darkness.

Today the sun is setting in New York at 4:29 p.m. I am in Florida with no need for a well-lit kitchen. Michele is in New York "enjoying the adventure" of being alive in the dark!

Darkness descends on our lives in many forms: illness, the death of a loved one, the termination of a relationship or a job. Sometimes it just covers our lives in a murky veil that obscures our vision and perspective. During these times the adventure can quickly deteriorate to a state of just getting by. It is important, however, to remember that the challenging words, "Life is a daring adventure or nothing at all" were written by Helen Keller, who was both blind and deaf. In her world of darkness and silence, Helen knew a great light. This light shone within her, but was also fanned into flame by her friend and companion, Annie Sullivan. Annie companioned Helen in her darkness and helped Helen to recognize her inner light of strength, hope, and courage. Annie Sullivan kept vigil with Helen until she could "see" the light, until she could own the light.

Why do so many of us sit in the darkness of our lives alone? Women are relational beings. We have so much to give to each other and so much to receive from one another. Annie could not give Helen the light, but she could point the way. She kept the watch—the vigil—as Helen bravely searched her soul and found her true self.

Being asked to keep vigil with someone is a wonderful gift. My niece, Alexandra, recently made her Confirmation. She asked me to be her sponsor, and I was very happy to participate in the ceremony. Just before the bishop began confirming the candidates, he spoke to the sponsors. His words were a powerful reminder of what it means to keep vigil. Each of us was told that the young person we were sponsoring had entrusted us with a very special role in their lives. We were being given the responsibility to watch with them and watch out for them throughout their life. We are to be vigil keepers of their faith. I left the church that afternoon with a much deeper appreciation of my role in Alexandra's life.

Some seasons of our lives are like winter, dark and cold, but we do not need to be alone. This might be a good time to gather your vigil keepers. Why not invite a friend or two to join you on a regular basis throughout this winter. Gather for tea or to share your thoughts on a book. Whatever you decide to do, make it a time when you are being there for one another, when you are keeping vigil for each other.

We can also call on the women who have gone before us to be our vigil keepers. What about a grandmother who has gone on to glory? Maybe it is time to invite her into the darkness of your winter. There are also the holy women who have touched our world in a larger way: St. Therese the Little Flower, St. Catherine of Siena, or Dorothy Day, to name a few. Through all these women we are surrounded with the strength, hope, and courage that was so much a part of their lives. They can keep the vigil and point the way for us. We only need to invite them in.

I would like to invite a wonderful woman who knew a great deal about darkness to be with us for a while. She is Mary, the Mother of Jesus. Raised as a Catholic, I heard many stories about Mary and was encouraged to emulate her. The problem was that it seemed impossible to be like her from the stories we heard. Let's think about it. Mary was conceived without original sin. Right there we differ. Add to that the fact that she was both virgin and mother. I believe the rest of us have to make an either/or choice! Mary was also assumed bodily into heaven after her death. Even as believers, it sure is hard to emulate someone who is so different from us.

These stories we've frequently heard about Mary only tell us half of the truth. Mary was also a young woman, about to be married, when God intervened. We know that she was frightened when an angel of God spoke to her. She hesitated before consenting to carry the Son of God. Of course she hesitated, her *yes* to God changed everything in her life!

Imagine being pregnant and unmarried and trying to explain to your parents and fiancée that an angel had appeared to you. How alone Mary must have felt. It was only when she met Elizabeth that someone embraced her with understanding. Elizabeth was a vigil keeper for Mary in her darkness. Throughout her whole life, Mary experienced many of the same emotions that we do. Frightened at the Annunciation, she was comforted by her visit to Elizabeth. The birth of Jesus brought her great joy, but there was an overshadowing of sadness when Simeon predicted the future of her child. At Cana, Mary was God's instrument to bring Jesus into his ministry. How many of you have found that you are the instruments guiding your children in their life's direction?

At the cross, Mary was heartbroken like every mother who has lost a child. These emotions expressed by Mary show us that she knows how we feel. She has walked the woman's journey and is always ready to be a vigil keeper for each of us. Why not invite Mary into your circle of women. She can model for us the way of faithfulness even in the darkness.

We await the light of Christmas, but not the historical event of Jesus' birth. We are waiting to be born anew in our *yes* to God. Time and eternity met two thousand years ago in Bethlehem, but they also meet each time one of us says "Yes" to being an instrument of God's love.

I would like to share with you a true Christmas story about a child who was born not too many years ago. A homeless family was living in a trailer at a beach campground. The woman's name was Mary and she was about to give birth. Early in the morning on December 25 the child was born and she was beautiful! A good woman named Nancy told me about the plight of this poor family, and I in turn told my Wednesday women's group about their situation. These women donated enough money to buy everything the baby would need, as well as gifts for her mother, father, and two-year-old brother. A circle of women gathered to help one who was in the darkness of poverty and homelessness. Nancy was the main vigil keeper, but we all supported Mary and her family.

The adventure of being alive is replete with struggles as well as joys; but being alive is much better than living as the "not yet dead." You must decide if this winter will be dark and dreary for you or a time of anticipation and celebration of the light. In the delightful book by C.S. Lewis, *The Lion, the Witch, and the Wardrobe*, we are told that the worst thing is for it to always be winter and never Christmas. Well, Christmas is almost here, so don't let the joy of the season pass you by as you rush around shopping, wrapping, and cooking. Rejoice that God cared enough for you to become flesh and bring the light of Divine Love into your life.

It is 4:45 p.m. in Florida and the sun has just slipped out of sight. I sit in its afterglow. In New York it is dark, and Michele waits for the new light. Maybe that is something we can all do as we live this adventure of being alive!

Merry Christmas!

Sister Pat

Soul Suggestions

Week One

Think about what you do when darkness descends into your life? Aside from chocolate, what are the tools that you use to sustain yourself? Do your tools need upgrading at the "God Depot?"

Week Two

Who are the "Elizabeths"—the vigil keepers—in your life? Send them a Christmas card from your soul.

Week Three

Take time this week to gather a group of winter vigil keepers. Set dates to meet as a circle of women.

Week Four

We are all called to be a vigil keepers like Annie Sullivan, Elizabeth, and Nancy. This week you are invited to reflect on ways you can sponsor or mentor other women in the adventure of being alive during the coming year.